THE FALL FEASTS OF ISRAEL

THE FALL FEASTS OF ISRAEL

by

Mitch and Zhava Glaser

MOODY PRESS
CHICAGO

To Jodee Steiner,
for help in typing
the manuscript

To Larry Brandt,
for help in research

© 1987 by
THE MOODY BIBLE INSTITUTE
OF CHICAGO

All Scripture quotations, unless noted otherwise, are from the *New American Standard Bible,* © 1960, 1962, 1963, 1968, 1971, 1972, 1973, 1975, and 1977 by The Lockman Foundation, and are used by permission.

Library of Congress Cataloging in Publication Data

Glaser, Mitch.
  The fall feasts of Israel / by Mitch and Zhava Glaser.
    p.   cm.
    Bibliography: p.
    ISBN 0-8024-2539-9
    1. Bible. O.T. Leviticus—Criticism, interpretation, etc.
2. Fasts and feasts in the Bible. 3. Fasts and feasts in the Bible—
Typology. 4. Rosh ha-Shanah. 5. Sukkoth. 6. Yom Kippur.
I. Glaser, Zhava. II. Title.
BS1255.2.G42 1987
222'.13064—dc19   87-17832
                                          CIP

9 10

Printed in the United States of America

Contents

Part 3: Sukkot

Introduction:

Jesus—Lord of the Calendar

1
Jesus—Lord of Time

In the beginning, God created time. He made light and darkness, calling the light day and the darkness night: "And there was evening and there was morning, one day" (Genesis 1:5). Yet the Holy One is eternal and lives beyond the limitations of time and space. He created time—the sequence of events—to serve as the arena where the heavenly meets the temporal, where God meets man. By His act of creation, the Sovereign of eternity was also crowned Lord of time.

The apostle John supplies additional knowledge on the Genesis record and tells us that the pre-incarnate Christ was the architect of creation. John wrote, "All things came into being by Him, and apart from Him nothing came into being that has come into being. In Him was life, and the life was the light of men. And the light shines in the darkness, and the darkness did not comprehend it" (John 1:3-5). The world of time and space were to become the special domain of the second Person of the Trinity. He is Creator, Redeemer, and King. Ultimately, His kingdom will include all that He has made, for heaven is His throne and the earth His footstool (Isaiah 66:1).

God intended events on earth to reflect heavenly realities. "Thy will be done, on earth as it is in heaven" (Matthew 6:10), Jesus taught us to pray. It is God's desire that our lives be characterized by heavenly values, that the temporal reflect the eternal. As God the Father ruled over the heavens, so man, created in His image, was to rule for Him on the earth. The natural beauty of the world declared the glory of God (Psalm 19:1), but that was not enough for the Lord of the universe. He desired that every man and woman reflect the beauty of His holiness through the moral quality of their lives. But that was not to be.

Early in history, Adam and Eve revolted and ripped away from God the mantle of leadership, enthroning themselves in His stead. Adam's rebellion would turn man's walk through history into a path of thorns. But God, moved by love for His creation, would not allow the anarchy to continue. Along with Adam's Fall and the judgment came a ray of divine hope in the promise of a Redeemer, a seed of the woman, who would conquer the rebels and restore the rightful Lord of time to His throne (Genesis 3:15). But until that wonderful day when Christ rules His creation, time remains a battlefield between good and evil.

The apostle Paul tells us to redeem the time, for the days are evil (Ephesians 5:16). The battle waged to redeem time, to sanctify our days as holy unto the Lord, is a critical one for believers in the Messiah. The day will surely come when every knee shall bow to Him (Philippians 2:10), but until then we must spend every moment in service worthy of the Lord.

The sanctity of time and the Lord's sovereignty over history were lessons that God sought to teach His chosen nation, Israel. Through the holy calendar given at Mount Sinai, the Lord of the Universe ordered the days of His people, focusing their attention on the heavenly realm. The feasts of the Lord were not given to enslave the Israelites but to free them to reflect on the Person, plan, and attributes of the Holy One of Israel. Through those special days, they were to recognize that He is Lord of every moment and must rule over every second of their lives.

The feasts and laws of the Lord were a tutor (Galatians 3:24) to lead the Israelites to the Savior. The apostle Paul described the Hebrew calendar as a "mere shadow" of what was to come. He wrote, "Therefore let no one act as your judge in regard to food or drink or in respect to a festival or a new moon or a sabbath day—things which are a mere shadow of what is to come; but the substance belongs to Christ" (Colossians 2:16-17). The apostle was not condemning those Jewish Christians who wished to continue celebrating the Jewish holidays. Rather, Paul asserted that the festivals lead to Christ.

It is appropriate, therefore, for a Jewish believer to celebrate these holidays in a way that is consistent with the apostolic faith and that exalts the Person of Jesus. Non-Jewish Christians as well must recognize that the festivals of Israel find their fulfillment in Christ and His new covenant. Jesus Himself said, "Do not think that I came to abolish the law or the prophets; I did not come to abolish but to fulfill" (Matthew 5:17). Christians who follow the church calendar will find that understanding the Levitical feasts adds a new depth and dimension to their lives. The feasts of Israel point to Jesus Christ as Lord of time and history.

In Leviticus 23, God calls the feasts of Israel "My appointed times." It was important for the Israelites to remember that behind the intricate details of each feast stood the God who ordained them, to remember that He created time, and to remember that history bears the image of His presence. The feasts of Israel were God's appointed times to remind His people that He was Lord of the calendar, the King of creation, and that He was to be worshiped every day. The feasts of the Lord have a great deal to teach all who have crowned Him Lord of their lives.

2
The Fall Feasts

The Hebrew Calendar

The traditional division of twelve months to the year is found in Scripture. In 1 Kings 4:7, the recorder of sacred history writes, "And Solomon had twelve deputies over all Israel, who provided for the King and his household; each man had to provide for a month in the year" (see also 1 Chronicles 27:2-15). The ancient Hebrews observed a twelve-month lunar year based on Psalm 104:19,[1] "He made the moon for the seasons; the sun knows the place of its setting."

The length of a lunar month, the period between two new moons, is 29 days, 12 hours, 44 minutes, and 2.8 seconds.[2] But the lunar calendar is 10 days and 21 hours shorter than the solar year.[3] If that discrepancy were not corrected, the order of the months would become so distorted that the Hebrews would be celebrating their spring holidays in the fall! To compensate, they instituted a periodic leap

---

1. S. Safrai and M. Stern, eds., *The Jewish People in the First Century*, vol. 2 (Philadelphia: Fortress, 1984), p. 835.
2. Ibid., p. 838. This calculation varies slightly according to the source. Alfred Edersheim claims the Jewish month has 29 days, 12 hours, 44 minutes, and 3.33 seconds and that the year consists of 354 days, 8 hours, 48 minutes, and 38 seconds (*The Temple: Its Ministry and Services* [Grand Rapids: Eerdmans, 1972], p. 200).
3. Victor Buksbazen, *The Gospel in the Feasts of Israel* (Fort Washington, Pa.: Christian Literature Crusade, 1954), p. 24.

year in which a thirteenth month was added after the twelfth month of Adar (roughly equivalent to March).

THE NEW MOON

The precise determination of the new moon has always been important to the Hebrews. Not knowing the exact time of the new moon could upset their entire calendar.

During the time of Christ, a confirmation of the day was made each month by a court of three people, which always included the high priest. They would gather in a special hall in the Temple and receive the testimony of "credible witnesses" who claimed to have seen the new moon. According to the Mishna,[4] not every witness was considered credible. The rabbis listed as ineligible: "a dice player, a usurer, those who fly pigeons, dealers in the produce of a Sabbatical year, and slaves." They continued, "This is the general principle: all evidence that a woman is not eligible to give, these also are not eligible to bring" (Rosh Hashanah 1:8). So it is doubtful that a woman's testimony was valid in the case of a new moon, although women were valid witnesses on other matters.

The Sanhedrin provided a sumptuous meal for this occasion to encourage witnesses to come forward. Once a new moon was confirmed, fires were lit on the Mount of Olives to notify those awaiting the signal on distant hills. The

---

4. The Mishna is the code of traditional Jewish law. It is also known as the Oral Torah. Orthodox Jews claim that the Mishna was given to Moses at Mount Sinai but was not written down until later. The name *Mishna* means repetition and comes from the way it was learned by the Jewish people. It was repeated and repeated until memorized. Between the second and fifth centuries, the Mishna and the commentary on the Mishna, the Gemara, were put in writing. But what was written down in the Mishna reflected a much earlier oral tradition. The Mishna is the best record available of the beliefs and practices of the Pharisees and their followers around the time of Christ.

message would flare from hill to hill beyond the boundaries of Israel, so that those in the Dispersion could know the new moon had appeared over the holy city. Precautions, though, had to be taken, because some of the enemies of the Jews would light fires to deceive those waiting for the message that the new moon had appeared. According to the Mishna, six witnesses of the new moon were dispatched in the months of Nisan (for Passover), Av (for the fast on account of the destruction of Jerusalem), Elul (because it preceded Tishri), Tishri (because of its holy festivals), Kislev (for Hanukkah), and Adar (for Purim; Rosh Hashanah 1:3). These dispatchers "hand-delivered" the message that the moon was new over Jerusalem.

The Hebrews sensed a holy obligation to live obediently before the Lord of time. If God had expressly designed a calendar, it was their duty to observe it properly. To the pious, it was no small thing if a new moon was mistaken and the appointed times of the Lord were observed on the wrong days. The Lord of the calendar was to be obeyed with heart-felt precision.

THE FEASTS

Leviticus 23 describes eight "appointed times" of the Lord (although the celebration of the new moon might have been included as well; Numbers 28:11-15). Along with the weekly Sabbath, seven periods in the Hebrew year were set apart as festivals or feasts. These were not feasts in the modern sense of banquets and revelry but were based on the sacrificial altar and the worship of God.

The feasts divide naturally into two groups. In the first group, all related to Passover, are the Paschal sacrifice, the feast of Unleavened Bread, the feast of First Fruits, and the Day of Pentecost. In the second group, all observed during Tishri, the sacred seventh month, we find the feast of Trumpets, the Day of Atonement, and the feast of Tabernacles. This study will concentrate on the last three—the fall feasts.

TISHRI—THE SEVENTH MONTH

The number *seven, symbolizing divine perfection,* is woven into the entire Hebrew calendar. The Sabbath is observed on the seventh day of the week, every seventh year is decreed a sabbatical year, and after seven sabbatical years a Jubilee year is observed. Seven weeks after Passover comes the celebration of the feast of Pentecost. The feast of Tabernacles, which completes the holiday season, lasts seven days. And the seventh month, Tishri, contains the most holy days of the Hebrew calendar. Today the feast of Trumpets and the Day of Atonement are called the "High Holy Days."

Tishri is the sabbatical month and, along with the seventh day of the week, was set apart as sacred. So the seventh month, the subject of this study, is the most holy of months.

THE THEMES OF THE FALL FEASTS

The fall feasts are unique among the appointed times of the Lord. The lessons they teach form a natural progression of thought: the feast of Trumpets teaches repentance; the Day of Atonement, redemption; and the feast of Tabernacles, rejoicing. On the feast of Trumpets, the sound of the ram's horn calls upon each Jew to repent and confess his sins before his Maker. The Day of Atonement is that ominous day when peace is made with God. On the feast of Tabernacles, Israel obeys God's command to rejoice over the harvest and the goodness of God. It is necessary to pass through repentance and redemption in order to experience His joy.

The themes of the fall feasts are especially meaningful to a believer in Jesus. The feasts—and the entire Old Testament—are fulfilled in Christ (Luke 24:26). We must repent of our sins before we can be forgiven by God, but repentance alone is not enough. Every Jew and Gentile must turn toward Christ, accepting His atoning sacrifice at Calvary and receiving Him in joy—unfathomable, everlasting, and indescribable—which this world cannot give or take away.

Our Path

It would be easier to study the fall feasts if modern Judaism religiously practiced the customs in Leviticus. But that is not the case. The feasts of Tishri have been reshaped and reformed over time. In every age, traditions, liturgy, and folklore have been added to their observance. By the time of Christ, every feast had already undergone significant changes when compared to its biblical foundations.

Changes continued after the Temple was destroyed in A.D. 70. In the early days of the second century, Jewish leaders struggled just to keep the feasts alive. Their task was to adapt the observance of the feasts to the sorrowful reality of the Temple's destruction.

The sacrificial altar had always been the focal point of the feasts. How has Judaism coped through the generations without it? How do Jewish people celebrate the feasts today?

To understand the feasts, we must first investigate what the Bible teaches about each of them, how they were observed in ancient times and in the time of Christ. We will also see how the feasts are celebrated today and will present the more classical beliefs and customs of Judaism. Our book depicts the way a practicing Jew would celebrate the "appointed times of the Lord." Yet we must keep in mind that for many modern Jews, the celebration of the festivals has been reduced to childhood memories. We should not presume that our Jewish friends observe the fall feasts exactly as presented in this book.

Understanding the fall festivals will enrich the lives and walks of believers in Christ. But we must not forget that Judaism is the religion of the rabbis. It is a religion based upon the Old Testament Scriptures, but it also incorporates centuries of Jewish interpretation and teaching. Tradition must not be confused with Scripture, or Judaism with biblical faith.

Nevertheless, as we learn about the fall feasts, we will gain insights into Jewish culture and be equipped to use the holidays to present the gospel to Jewish friends. The feasts of Israel are fulfilled in Jesus, for the entirety of the Old Covenant points to Him, the Lord of the calendar and Master of all.

Part 1:

Rosh Hashanah

3

The Biblical Institution
of Rosh Hashanah

A REMINDER BY BLOWING OF TRUMPETS

The seventh month of the Jewish calendar clearly stood out above the others in the eyes of Moses and Israel. As God announced the order of the Hebrew calendar, He instructed the people to punctuate the arrival of each new month with a celebration and a blowing of trumpets. But He emphasized the seventh month when from the foot of Mount Sinai He said through Moses the lawgiver: "In the seventh month on the first of the month, you shall have a rest, a reminder by blowing of trumpets, a holy convocation" (Leviticus 23:24).

So a feast was decreed on the first of the seventh month. But what was it to be called? When He gave the calendar, God Himself named the appointed feasts—the Sabbath, the Passover, the Day of Atonement. But this feast received no title. It was simply "Yom T'ruah"—the day of blowing. So it became the feast of Trumpets. And the blowing of the trumpets became the distinguishing characteristic of the day, calling the people's attention to the awesome festival that was to follow—the Day of Atonement.

A SABBATH REST

On the first of Tishri at the call of the shofar, an instrument made from a ram's curved horn, all "servile" work was to cease. This set the feast of Trumpets apart from the first day of other Hebrew months. The restrictions were not as stringent as those on the weekly Sabbath or the Day of Atonement, but regular duties and everyday jobs could not be carried out. The preoccupations of daily life receded into the background as all thoughts turned to the days ahead, to the coming Day of Atonement.

The blowing of the shofar was a memorial, but a memorial of what? The Scriptures do not say. Certainly the call of the shofar reminded Israel that the seventh month had begun. It was distinctive from that of the silver trumpets blown on other new moons. Silver trumpets were sounded at the daily burnt offering and at the beginning of each new month (Numbers 10:10), but the shofar specifically was blown on the beginning of the month of Tishri. (The silver trumpets were probably blown as well [Bab. Rosh Hashanah 26b], however, as it was also a new moon.)

THE SHOFAR

The shofar has always held a prominent role in the history of God's ancient people. Rabbis have delighted in quoting its long history of biblical usage: "The shofar was created for the welfare of Israel. The Torah was given to Israel with the sound of the shofar [Exodus 19:19]. Israel conquered in the battle of Jericho with the blast of the shofar [Joshua 6:20]. Israel will be advised of the advent of the Messiah with the sound of the shofar [Zechariah 9:14]. And the Holy One, blessed be He, will sound the shofar at the time of the ingathering of the exiles of Israel to their place [Isaiah 27:13]" (Eliyahu Zuta 2).

In the Bible record, the shofar was blown to signal the assembly of the Israelites during war (Judges 3:27; 2 Samuel 20:1). The sound gripped the hearts of women and children with fear, as their men were called away to battle and to an unknown fate. The watchmen that stood upon Jerusalem's walls blew the shofar to warn the people of impending danger (Amos 3:6; Jeremiah 6:1; Ezekiel 33:6).

But the shofar did not always strike a fearful note. The shofar was also blown at the start of the Jubilee year (Leviticus 25:9), the great sabbatical release provided by God. Eagerly the slaves and hopelessly indebted listened for the joyful sound that signaled their freedom! The land itself welcomed the trumpet blast that allowed it to rest.

The accession of a new king to the throne was announced by the shofar's voice (1 Kings 34:39). What a time of feasting and pageantry for Israel!

The shofar's call is a reminder to the Jewish people that God is sovereign: "God has ascended with a shout, the Lord with the sound of a trumpet" (Psalm 47:5).

The Scriptures also predict the role of the shofar in the future restoration of Israel. Isaiah envisioned the shofar blast as announcing the gathering of dispersed Israel: "It will come about also in that day that a great trumpet will be blown; and those who were perishing in the land of Assyria and who were scattered in the land of Egypt will come and worship the Lord in the holy mountain at Jerusalem" (Isaiah 27:13).

Similarly, Zechariah writes that the Lord Himself will blow the shofar on the day when He delivers His people from attacking heathen armies: "Then the Lord will appear over them, and His arrow will go forth like lightning; and the Lord God will blow the trumpet, and will march in the storm winds of the south" (Zechariah 9:14).

The shofar called Israel to attention, to fear and trembling, to rejoicing; but at the feast of Trumpets, the sound of the shofar beckoned the people with a message unlike any other: a message of a Sabbath rest, a holy convocation, a time to present special burnt offerings to the Lord.

Traditionally, the sounding of the shofar has been a memorial for the Jewish people of God's faithfulness to Abraham. The ram's horn is a reminder of Abraham's sacrifice of Isaac and God's provision of a ram as a substitute.

Perhaps the shofar blast was intended to remind the Hebrews of the awesome event of the giving of the law and their promised obedience (Exodus 19:8). Thus, the shofar was an exclamation mark reminding Israel of God's faithfulness to Abraham and of the faithfulness God required of them.

THE OFFERINGS OF THE FEAST

The people of Israel offered sacrificial animals at the beginning of each new month. But on the seventh month, Yom T'ruah required an additional set of festal sacrifices besides the new moon and regular daily offerings.

The specific offerings recorded in Numbers 29:4 on Yom T'ruah are one bullock, one ram, seven he-lambs with the proper meal offerings, together with a he-goat for a sin-offering. That is similar to the sacrifices prescribed for the usual new moon celebration (Numbers 28:11-15). But the Yom T'ruah offerings were to be presented in addition to the offerings of the new month and the regularly scheduled daily offerings.

THE FEAST OF TRUMPETS IN BIBLICAL HISTORY

From the giving of the law at Sinai until the return of the Babylonian captives, there is no mention in the Bible of the feast of Trumpets. We cannot assume from the silence of the Scriptures that the feast was not celebrated, but there is an interesting passage that adds credence to that view.

Under the leadership of King Josiah, Israel underwent a spiritual renewal. When the Scriptures were found hidden away in the Temple, Josiah charged Hilkiah the priest:

"Go, inquire of the Lord . . . concerning the words of the book which has been found; for great is the wrath of the Lord which is poured out on us because our fathers have not observed the word of the Lord to do according to all that is written in this book" (2 Chronicles 34:21).

By Josiah's own admission, the observance of God's Word and the attendant holidays had been grossly neglected. This righteous king's zeal for the Lord inspired a revival in Israel, but even so there was no mention of the celebration of Yom T'ruah; only of the feast of Passover (2 Chronicles 34:31).

The Babylonian captivity, which lasted seventy years, was the direct result of Israel's neglect of the sabbatical year (2 Chronicles 36:20-21)—one year of captivity for each Sabbath year unobserved. A bit of mathematics yields the harsh truth about the spiritual condition of Israel—they had ignored the Scripture's commands for 490 years!

ISRAEL AFTER THE EXILE

The exiles who returned to Israel under the leadership of Ezra and Nehemiah were repentant and willing to obey God. The holy altar was finally restored on the first day of the seventh month (Ezra 3:5), and the people immediately began sacrificing to the Lord. This was likely a celebration of the feast of Trumpets, yet the call of the shofar was conspicuously missing. Perhaps the Israelites had forgotten the command during the captivity, or maybe they did not fully understand the importance of the seventh-month feasts. Whatever the reason, the blowing of the shofar was not mentioned.

On the first of Tishri, Ezra publicly read and translated the Scriptures (Nehemiah 8:8). It was no mere ritual observance—the people hungered to know God's Word. Hearing the sacred commandments, they realized how far their nation had strayed from His holy precepts, and their hearts were rent with anguish (Nehemiah 8:9). Yet Ezra put a stop to the grievous display. He encouraged the people, saying, "Go, eat of the fat, drink of the sweet, and send portions to him who has nothing prepared; for this day is holy to our Lord. Do not be grieved, for the joy of the Lord is your strength" (Nehemiah 8:10).

The people were not to grieve but to rejoice! God had forgiven their transgressions and restored them to the land of their forefathers. Curiously enough, the sober themes of repentance and judgment, which would become the backbone of rabbinic teaching on the holiday, are totally absent from the scene. It seems probable, however, that the event being described is indeed the observance of the feast of Trumpets. It could not have been the Day of Atonement, as Yom Kippur was a day when God had commanded them to afflict their souls. It could not have been the feast of Booths, because it was not until the second day of their feast (it would seem that the feast of Trumpets was celebrated for two days) that they realized God had commanded them to celebrate the feast of Booths. The evidence points to this festival's being the feast of Trumpets.

SCRIPTURAL ALLUSIONS TO THE FEAST OF TRUMPETS

The themes and symbols of the feast found their way into the works of the biblical authors.

In Psalm 81 we read, "Sing for joy to God our strength; shout joyfully to the God of Jacob. . . . Blow the trumpet at the new moon, at the full moon, on our feast day, for it is a statute for Israel, an ordinance of the God of Jacob" (Psalm 81:1, 3).

Both phrases, "shout joyfully to the God of Jacob" and "blow the trumpet," are built on the same Hebrew word, *T'ruah,* meaning to make a loud noise. It is the same word God used in connection with sounding the shofar when commanding the observance of the feast at Mount Sinai.

The blowing of the ram's horn is linked here to the observance of the new month, but as it is also called a feast day, the psalmist was likely referring to the feast of Trumpets.

The psalmist goes on to tell of God's faithfulness to Israel and their faithlessness in return. When the Israelites called on God, He rescued them (v. 7), but they did not obey when God called to them (v. 11). Yet God continued to call upon Israel to repent, that He might bless and provide for them (v. 16). On the feast of Trumpets, God reminded His people of His faithfulness and called them back to Himself in repentance.

The prophet Isaiah also spoke of the shofar's cry being a call to repentance, as the Lord proclaims through him, "Cry loudly, do not hold back; raise your voice like a trumpet, and declare to My people their transgression, and to the house of Jacob their sins" (Isaiah 58:1).

The blowing of the shofar calls the Israelite to behold the justice and mercy of God, that he may know Him and walk in His presence: "How blessed are the people who know the joyful sound! O Lord, they walk in the light of Thy countenance. In Thy name they rejoice all the day. And by Thy righteousness they are exalted" (Psalm 89:15-16).

Only in the "light of His countenance," relying on His mercy, can we fulfill our obligation to turn from sin. The rabbis teach, "Happy is the people that understands how to conciliate their Creator with the blast of the shofar" (Pesikta Rabbati). May the piercing tones of the ram's horn lead the Jewish people and all people to repentance and reconciliation with the God of Abraham.

4

Rosh Hashanah
in the Time of Christ

Though the feast of Trumpets had been neglected, by the time of Christ, Rosh Hashanah was once again faithfully observed. In fact, it was considered the second most solemn day of the Jewish year. The themes that were prominent in Old Testament revelation—repentance, restoration, judgment, and sovereignty—had been incorporated into the pharisaic teachings on the feast and were well-known throughout the Diaspora.

The blowing of the shofar, absent in Ezra's time, was now more important than ever. Since the Israelites, by now widely scattered, were not required to travel to Jerusalem for the feast of Rosh Hashanah, the blowing of the shofar took on added significance in the synagogues of the Dispersion.

The feast was important because of its primary role in the Jewish calendar and its spiritual significance preceding the Day of Atonement. The Mishna is a major source of information about it, for the laws and discussions of the rabbis reflect the celebration of the holiday at the time of Christ.

THE FOUR NEW YEARS

Rosh Hashanah means "The Head of the Year," yet the Bible places it in the seventh month, not the first. When did the feast of Trumpets come to be regarded as the Jewish New Year?

Nowhere in Scripture is the first of Tishri called "Rosh Hashanah" or the "New Year." Rather, God decreed that Nisan should be the first month (Exodus 12:2). Traditionally, though, the feast of Trumpets has been interpreted as the Jewish New Year. The Hebrew phrase "Rosh Hashanah" is used only once in the Bible, by the prophet Ezekiel, who wrote during the Babylonian exile: "In the twenty-fifth year of our exile, at the beginning of the year [Rosh Hashanah], on the tenth of the month, in the fourteenth year after the city was taken, on that same day the hand of the Lord was brought upon me and brought me there" (40:1).

The vision of the Temple that follows does not give us any clue as to whether Ezekiel was referring to the month of Nisan or Tishri. Yet there is some evidence that before the time of Moses, Tishri was thought to be the first month of the year. Some ancient sources speak of the new year's beginning with the fall harvest. An ancient farmer's calendar unearthed at Gezer marks the succession of months in relation to the various duties a farmer had to perform in the course of a year. The calendar begins in the fall season with the initial task of "gathering in the crops."[1]

Two phrases used of the feast of Tabernacles add weight to this position, as the feast (in Tishri) is said to have taken place "at the end of the year" (Exodus 23:16). Tishri would thus serve both as the conclusion and beginning of the ancient calendar.

Throughout the ages, Judaism has maintained a distinction between the religious and the civil year. Even to-

---

1. Abraham P. Bloch, *The Biblical and Historical Background of the Jewish Holy Days* (New York: KTAV, 1978), pp. 18-19.

day, the month of Nisan and the feast of Passover begin the religious year of the Jews, yet Tishri and Rosh Hashanah begin the civil year. Many Jewish writers trace this system of two new years to the Babylonian captivity. Others say the distinction existed since the time of Moses, when God set aside Nisan as the first month of the religious year[2] (Exodus 12:2).

However, Rosh Hashanah was not the only "new year" observed by the Jewish people. The Mishna declared that God had established four new years:

The first of Nisan was the new year for kings and for festivals. No matter when a Jewish king ascended to the throne, the initial year of his reign would conclude on the first of Nisan, even if he had ruled for only one day. Nisan began the religious year for feasts because God had declared Passover to be first among His "appointed times."

The first of Elul was the new year for animals.

The first of Tishri was called the new year "for the years, for sabbatical years, for Jubilee years, for planting and for vegetables." Agriculture was the main economic activity of the ancient Hebrews, and so the month's association with planting made it first in the "fiscal" year, though it was later given spiritual significance as well.

The first of Shevat was the new year for trees, according to the school of Shammai, although the school of Hillel said this was on the fifteenth. The opinion of the school of Hillel became the accepted view (Rosh Hashanah 1:1).

By the time of Christ, the identification of the seventh month, Tishri, and especially Rosh Hashanah, as the be-

2. Edersheim, p. 295.

ginning of the fiscal year was already well-established, as was the observance of Passover as the beginning of the religious year. Those distinctions remain until the present.

THE SECOND DAY OF ROSH HASHANAH

In the time of Christ, as today, Rosh Hashanah was celebrated on not one day but two. One Talmudic tradition claims that the second day was added during the time of the early prophets and the monarchy (Jerusalem; Erubin 3). A divergent view suggests that the second day began to be observed in Babylon.

According to the Talmud, the high priest, as religious head of the community, had absolute authority to proclaim the new moon. The rabbis write that in Babylon, when Ezekiel and his disciples assumed the religious leadership, the declaration became a judicial act similar to the pronouncement of a verdict by a court of law (Sanhedrin 11b). All judgments, of course, had to be based on legal evidence, and thus it became the custom to proclaim the new moon on the testimony of a witness. The additional day of Rosh Hashanah, then, was established to give the courts a day to evaluate the testimony of the witnesses. By the first century, the duty had once again passed to the high priest, but according to Jewish law, he was still required to receive the testimony of witnesses before he could declare a new moon.

THE FOUR JUDGMENTS

The role of Rosh Hashanah in the judgment of Israel and the Gentiles (based upon Deuteronomy 11:13-18) was greatly expanded by the time of Christ. The rabbis believed that God had determined four seasons of judgment for the world. The judgment of God was often expressed in agricultural terms, as He withheld or blessed the nation's crops. Thus: "The world is judged at four periods in the year: on Passover, for grain [Passover was the time of the barley harvest], on the festival of Weeks, for the fruit of trees [Pentecost began the fruit season]."

The rabbis say, "On the new year, all the inhabitants of the world pass before Him like flocks of sheep, as it is said, 'He who fashioneth the hearts of them all, who understandeth all their doings' " (Rosh Hashanah 1:2).

The Gemara[3] comments on this, telling of three books that are opened in the heavenly courts during the feast of Rosh Hashanah:

> Three books are opened on Rosh Hashanah, one for the completely righteous, one for the completely wicked, and one for the average persons. The completely righteous are immediately inscribed in the book of life. The completely wicked are immediately inscribed in the book of death. The average persons are kept in suspension from Rosh Hashanah to the Day of Atonement. If they deserve well, they are inscribed in the book of life; if they do not deserve well, they are inscribed in the book of death.

Those in the "in-between" category—most of mankind—were given the ten days between Rosh Hashanah and Yom Kippur to repent. This view is attributed to third-century Rabbi Yochanan, who wrote in Rosh Hashanah 16b. A late second-century sage, Rabbi Meir, contested the viewpoint of those rabbis who believed in four periods of judgment. Rabbi Meir insisted that all judgments are passed on Rosh Hashanah (Rosh Hashanah 16a).

---

3. Taken from the Aramaic word for "completion," the Gemara is a collection of commentaries on the Mishna by the rabbis of Jerusalem and Babylonia during the third through fifth centuries of the Christian era. It includes the law, folklore, Bible commentary, science, theology, and legends of classical Judaism. The Gemara and Mishna, when published together, are called the Talmud.

But Rabbi Meir's was a minority opinion, which, although emphasizing the importance of Rosh Hashanah, detracted from the significance of the Day of Atonement.

The concept of the books of judgment is based on two Scripture passages. Psalm 69:28 says, "May they be blotted out of the Book of Life, and may they not be recorded with the righteous," and Exodus 32:32-33 says, " 'But now, if thou wilt, forgive their sin—and if not, please blot me out from Thy book which Thou has written!' And the Lord said to Moses, 'Whoever has sinned against me, I will blot him out of My book.' "

The fourth period of judgment is the feast of Tabernacles. The Mishna says, "And on the Festival of Tabernacles, they are judged for water" (Rosh Hashanah 1:2).

This again is a reference to the agricultural life-style of the Israelites. Tabernacles was the time of the latter rains and was the subject of great prayer and concern. Since the Israelite crops depended on rain, ceremonies were instituted to assure the people that God would grant it in abundance.

The judgment on Rosh Hashanah is unique, though, in that its character is universal: God takes note of the sins of all mankind. Each inhabitant of the world, by himself and not as a part of any nation, passes before God. This is quite different from the other judgments, which are limited to the Jewish nation.

THE BLOWING OF THE SHOFAR

The traditions surrounding the blowing of the shofar had developed significantly by the time of Christ. The rabbis had intricate regulations regarding its appearance and use.

The Mishna states, "All kinds of shofar are valid except that of a cow" (Rosh Hashanah 3:2). It would certainly have been unwise to use a cow's horn and remind God of the sin of the golden calf. Instead, the ram's horn was used and served as a reminder of the ram that God substituted for the sacrifice of Isaac.

The Mishna forbade the use of any shofar that was not in perfect condition. Already, special significance had been given to the tone of the shofar. The rabbis in the New Testament period were concerned about the type of sound the instrument produced and so forbade the use of an imperfect instrument.

The shofar could be carved but not painted, and it was preferable that it be bent or curved, as a reminder of the attitude of contrition one ought to have before the Lord at this season. It was to be splendid in its decoration and especially set apart for use on Rosh Hashanah.

The ceremony of the blowing of the shofar during the time of Christ was magnificent to see and experience. The priest chosen to blow the shofar was trained for his calling since youth; he was an artist, a virtuoso of sacred song. On Rosh Hashanah, he would raise the twisted horn and press his lips to the golden mouthpiece, draw an enormous breath of air, and begin to blow. The haunting sound of the horn would pierce through the Temple mount, stirring the hearts of the faithful in dire need of repentance. Three times the shofar would sound, followed by the blast of silver trumpets blown by two attending priests. The sound of those trumpets was a mere echo of the mournful call of the ram's horn.

On a fast day, the Mishna records that the mouthpiece of the shofar was overlaid with silver, and the priest blowing the shofar stood on the outside with two trumpeters. The trumpets blew the long blast and the shofar the shorter (Rosh Hashanah 3:4). This comparison once again reveals the central role of the shofar on New Year's Day.

THE HEARING OF THE SHOFAR BLAST

The rabbis declared it a religious duty to hear the call of the shofar. After all, how could the blast of the ram's horn pierce the soul and provoke repentance if a man did not hear it? An open ear to the shofar's call was a sign of an open heart to its stirring message.

The Mishna actually prescribed the level of concentration that was required of a man upon hearing the shofar.

> If one were passing behind a synagogue, or if his house were close to a synagogue, and he heard the sound of the shofar, or the reading of the megillah (the roll of Esther read on the feast of Purim), if he concentrated his mind on it, he has performed his duty, but if not, he has not carried out his obligation. (Rosh Hashanah 3:7)

An incidental hearing of the shofar blast on Rosh Hashanah would not suffice. If someone merely heard the echo of the shofar, the rabbis said he had not fulfilled his religious duty to actually hear the shofar itself (Rosh Hashanah 3:7). Only a concentrated effort and intentional availing of the ear would fulfill one's duty to God.

The Mishna reminds us of the time when Moses held up his hands to give victory in battle to the Israelites. It was not his raised hands that gave them victory, as the rabbis wrote: "This is rather to teach that whenever Israel looked on high and subjected their heart to their Father in heaven, they prevailed, but if not they fell" (Rosh Hashanah 3:7).

And when those who had been bitten by the snakes looked in faith upon the brazen serpent and were healed, it was not the serpent but God in heaven who healed: "Only, whenever Israel looked on high and subjected their heart to their Father in heaven were they healed, but if not, they perished" (Rosh Hashanah 3:7).

The noise emanating from the shofar does not cause a man to repent. Only when an individual Israelite looked into his own heart and then heavenwards to God would the Holy One act in his favor.

These passages in the Mishna give us insight into the essence of the Pharisaic religion.[4] Their perceptions are remarkable and should remind us that Pharisaism was not always a cold and legalistic religion. The apostle Paul wrote that many in Israel had a "zeal for God," but it was "not in accordance with knowledge" (Romans 10:2). The duty of hearing the shofar was not fulfilled until it pierced the soul and brought a man to his moral senses.

THE THEMES OF ROSH HASHANAH

The writers of the Mishna name three types of shofar blasts:

> The manner of sounding is three, of three each. The length of the sustained note is the same as three quavering notes. The length of a quavering note is equal to that of three wailing notes. If one sounded the first sustained note and then prolonged the second sustained note for as long as two it counts only as one. If one had already recited the benediction, then happened to obtain a shofar, he should sound three times a sustained note, a quavering note and a sustained note. (Rosh Hashanah 4:9)

The three blasts represented the three major themes of Rosh Hashanah: sovereignty (*malchuyot*), remembrance (*zichronot*), and the sound of the shofar (*shofarot*).

It was recorded, "They must not recite less than ten verses about sovereignty, ten verses of remembrance, and ten *shofarot* verses" (Rosh Hashanah 4:6). It is curious that these Scripture verses may not mention divine pun-

4. Edersheim, p. 299.

ishment. One noted Jewish writer says, "Such verses would not be consonant with the character of Rosh Hashanah. Its supplications are addressed to the mercy of God."[5] The emphasis on Rosh Hashanah is not upon judgment but rather on *averting* judgment by repenting and appealing to God's mercy.

Each of these themes is further developed in rabbinic thought and liturgy, but as early as the first century, all three held great meaning:

Sovereignty is a reference to the kingdom of God, for on Rosh Hashanah the Jewish people affirm God as King over Israel and over the world. Through repentance we become His righteous subjects.

Remembrance is an appeal to God to remember His covenant with Israel and a similar appeal to man to repent of his sin and obey God.

Shofarot, the blowing of the shofar, recalls the scriptural instances of the shofar's sounding.

A series of benedictions recited by the worshiper on Rosh Hashanah was possibly distilled from the liturgy of the second Temple. The rabbis of the Mishna disagreed about the order of the benedictions, but from their discussions we can draw an expanded list of the festival themes at the time of Christ:

> The order of the blessings: one recites the Patriarchs, the Powers, the Holiness of God's Name and includes with them Sovereignty, but one does not sound, the Holiness of the Day and one does not sound, the Remembrance and one does not sound, the Shofarot and one

5. Philip Blackman, ed., *Mishnayoth* (Gateshead: Judaica Press, 1977), p. 402.

does not sound, and he recites the Temple service, and the thanksgiving and the priestly blessings. (Rosh Hashanah 4:5)

THE INFLUENCE OF ROSH HASHANAH

It is difficult to discern how much influence Rosh Hashanah had on Israel's religious life during the time of Christ. There is no clear description of a Rosh Hashanah celebration in the Temple, but we know it was observed both there and in the synagogues of the Diaspora. In fact, we know that once during the morning Temple service the shofar was blown, and the Roman soldiers mistakenly thought it was a signal for revolt. The Roman armies then massacred hundreds of Jews. Because of that, the rabbis ordained that the shofar be blown later during the additional service (Musaf).[6] That incident leaves no doubt that the shofar was blown on Rosh Hashanah during the time of Christ.

THE NEW TESTAMENT AND ROSH HASHANAH

There is no mention in the New Testament that Jesus observed the feast. Since males were not required by law to go to Jerusalem on Rosh Hashanah, we would not expect Jesus to be present. Neither do we see Him in Jerusalem on the Day of Atonement. The New Testament writers, though, were familiar with the themes and activities of the season, and a number of passages allude to Rosh Hashanah observance.

In Matthew, Jesus tells His disciples that a trumpet would herald the new age:

> But immediately after the tribulation of those days the sun will be darkened, and the moon will not give its light,

6. Ibid., p. 403.

and the stars will fall from the sky, and the powers of the heavens will be shaken, and then the sign of the Son of Man will appear in the sky, and then all the tribes of the earth will mourn, and they will see the Son of Man coming on the clouds of the sky with power and great glory. And He will send forth His angels with a great [*shofar*] and they will gather together His elect from the four winds, from one end of the sky to the other. (Matthew 24:29-31)

This regathering of the faithful occurs in the context of judgment and restoration, themes of Rosh Hashanah. The judgment of God is poured out upon Israel for her sins:

And it will come about in all the land, declares the Lord, that two parts in it will be cut off and perish; but the third will be left in it. And I will bring the third part through the fire, refine them as silver is refined, and test them as gold is tested. They will call on My name, and I will answer them. I will say, they are My people, and they will say the Lord is my God. (Zechariah 13:8-9)

God will not destroy the elect. Rather, He will refine and restore His faithful ones. The blowing of the shofar symbolized to the Jewish mind the process of God's judgment, Israel's repentance, and divine restoration.

The apostle Paul spoke to the Thessalonians about the end times, the fate of their believing dead, and the role of death and resurrection in the life of the believer: "For the Lord Himself will descend from heaven with a shout, with the voice of the archangel and with the [*shofar*] of God; and the dead in Christ shall rise first" (1 Thessalonians 4:16).

Believers will once again see their loved ones who have died in the faith. The dead in Christ will be resurrected before the living meet the Lord in the air (1 Thessalonians 4:17). This regathering will also be announced by the

shofar of God. It was already common Jewish teaching that
the shofar would announce the resurrection of the dead.
Although judgment was central to the passage in Matthew,
it was not so with the Thessalonian believers. The message
of the apostle Paul is a word of comfort reminding the
Thessalonian Christians that God would remember His
new covenant and regather His new people to Himself.

Finally, the apostle John records the blowing of the
seventh trumpet in Revelation (11:15-18). John heard loud
voices in heaven saying, "The kingdom of the world has become the kingdom of our Lord, and of His Christ; and He
will reign forever and ever" (Revelation 11:15). Here we
see the blowing of the trumpet linked with the theme of
malchuyot, or sovereignty. For ultimately, God will recap-
ture the rebellious world and restore His sovereignty through
Jesus, His appointed regent. After judgment upon judgment
is poured out, Christ will sovereignly reclaim His world and
establish His throne in the holy city.

5
Jewish Observance of Rosh Hashanah

Rosh Hashanah, the Jewish New Year, is not ushered in with parties and revelry like the civil new years of secular societies. According to Jewish tradition, the New Year is a time of solemn self-evaluation. On Rosh Hashanah, those who are found wholly righteous are written in the Book of Life, the wholly wicked in the Book of Death, and the undetermined ones, most of mankind, are held in the balance for the next ten days, until the Day of Atonement. Then the Books of Judgment are sealed, and the sentence decreed for the year cannot be changed.

A SEASON OF INTROSPECTION

Rosh Hashanah is a time of introspection when pious Jews attempt to weight the heavenly balance in their favor, that they might be inscribed for life and a prosperous year ahead.

Judaism teaches that man was created with both a good inclination (*yetzer ha-tov*) and an evil inclination (*yetzer ha-ra*). Each man must choose to obey God's law rather than follow his evil tendencies and reap judgment. A man's righteous deeds could offset his evil deeds. A thorough, sincere repentance could make up for an entire life lived in sin. By the Day of Atonement, it was imperative that the scale be tipped in favor of the good to assure a positive judgment.

The rabbis issued a stern warning that a man should always regard himself as though he were half guilty and half righteous, since every one of his deeds had lasting value. One good deed could outweigh a multitude of evil ones, and likewise one evil action could negate a lifetime of good works.

Rabbi Simeon ben Yohai said: "Even if he is perfectly righteous all his life but rebels at the end, he destroys his former good deeds, for it is said, 'The righteousness of the righteous shall not deliver him in the day of his transgression' (Ezekiel 33:12a). And even if one is completely wicked all his life but repents at the end, he is not reproached with his wickedness, for it is said, 'and as for the wickedness of the wicked, he shall not fall thereby in the day that he turneth from his wickedness' " (Ezekiel 33:12b; Kiddushin 40a-b).

The Preparation for the Feast

So important is this high holy day season that spiritual preparation for it is begun a month in advance, with the start of the sixth month, Elul. According to Jewish tradition, Moses went up to Mount Sinai to receive the second tablets of the law on the first day of Elul, remained there for forty days, and descended to a forgiven people on the Day of Atonement. Since then, the days of Elul have been consecrated as days of repentance.

Emotionally and psychologically, the month of Elul is intended to set the tone for repentance during the coming Days of Awe; for repentance does not come easily but must be carefully cultivated. During the period of Elul, many Jewish people visit the graves of deceased relatives to gain inspiration from their lives for the coming year.

The mood of the high holiday season heightens, as special prayers of repentance and supplication (Selichot) are recited the entire week before Rosh Hashanah. Pious Jews wake up early to pray heart-wrenching prayers. Many also attend the *mikvah*, or public bath, for ritual cleansing on the day before Rosh Hashanah.

THE MOOD OF THE FEAST

The Jewish worshiper passes through many different moods on Rosh Hashanah. On one hand, this holiday is the Day of Judgment when his future hangs in the balance between life and death. On the other hand, it is New Year's Day—the day, the rabbis tell us, of the creation of the world, and it should be a joyous occasion as well.

How did the rabbis deduce that Rosh Hashanah was the Lord's day of judgment? Jewish tradition believes that Adam was created on this day (Sanhedrin 38b). And how did they decide that this was the day of the year the world was created? Because the first word of the Torah is *Bereshit* ("in the beginning"), and when changed around it reads *Aleph b'Tishri* ("On the first of Tishri") God created the heaven and the earth.[1] Wasn't it logical to assume that man would be judged on the anniversary of his creation?

According to tradition, Adam sinned and was forgiven, all on the first day of his creation. The first man was then told by God, "Just as you stood before me in judgment on this day and came out free, so your children, who will stand before me in judgment on this day, will be set free" (Vayikra Rabba 29:1).

Another tradition, that the sacrifice of Isaac took place on Rosh Hashanah, provided even more reason for the rab-

1. Richard Siegel, Sharon Strassfeld, and Michael Strassfeld, *The Jewish Catalog* (Philadelphia: Jewish Publication Society of America, 1973), p. 122.

bis to believe this was the day of judgment: "The offspring of Isaac will someday transgress my will, and I will judge them on Rosh Hashanah. Should they appeal to my leniency, I will recall the binding of Isaac and let them blow then the horn of this ram [which was substituted for Isaac]" (Tanchuma, Vayero 22:13).

As we can see from these passages, the rabbis express confidence in God's mercy. For even though a man is judged on Rosh Hashanah, he should be confident that just as God forgave Adam and spared the life of Isaac, he too will gain a favorable decree before his Maker (Tanchuma, Vayero 22:13).

The Evening Service

Traditionally, the Jewish day is reckoned from evening to evening, so the synagogue service on the eve of Rosh Hashanah actually initiates the holiday. The mood of the worshipers on this night is festive, not mournful, but the tone of the liturgy is serious. On this night, the prayers are not chanted in their usual melodies, but rather with the intonations of the Days of Awe. The ear of the worshiper can discern these mournful melodies that call his attention to the sober days ahead.

The synagogue service takes a melancholy turn as the ark of the Torah is opened and the chant of *Un'saneh Tokef* begins. Pious worshipers pull their prayer shawls over their heads and with tears and sobs recite the words of God's judgment upon them, for on this day will be determined: "How many are to pass away, and how many are to come into existence; who are to live and who are to die . . . who shall have repose and who shall be troubled . . . who shall be cast down and who shall be exalted."[2]

2. Hayyim Schauss, *The Jewish Festivals: History and Observance*, trans. Samuel Jaffe (New York: Schocken, 1975), p. 148.

Yet in spite of this awesome decree, the Jewish person reassures himself that he can earn God's blessing and avert His judgment by doing sufficient good deeds.

THE BLOWING OF THE SHOFAR

Though the recounting of God's judgment is an emotional moment, it is not at all the central point of the service. This exalted moment comes when the shofar is sounded, calling the people to repentance.

So central is this moment to Rosh Hashanah that the rabbis even speculated that the very redemption of Israel would come through the ram's horn: "The Holy One, blessed be He, said to Abraham: 'Your children are destined to be caught by the nations and entangled in troubles . . . but they will ultimately be redeemed through the horns of the ram' " (Leviticus Rabbah 29:10).

As with many other significant Jewish customs, there were many interpretations of the blowing of the shofar; so many, in fact, that in the ninth century, Saadia Gaon, a leading Babylonian rabbi and scholar, codified the ten main reasons it is blown on the feast of Trumpets:

1. Trumpets are sounded at a coronation and God is hailed as King on this day.
2. The shofar heralds the beginning of a penitential season (from Rosh Hashanah to the Day of Atonement).
3. The Torah was given on Sinai accompanied by blasts of the shofar.
4. The prophets compare their message to the sound of the shofar.
5. The conquering armies that destroyed the Temple sounded trumpet blasts.
6. The ram was substituted for Isaac.
7. The prophet asks: "If a trumpet is blown in a city, will not the people tremble?" (Amos 3:6).

8. The prophet Zephaniah speaks of the great "day of
   the Lord" (Judgment Day) as a "day of trumpet and
   battle cry" (Zephaniah 1:14, 16).
9. The prophet Isaiah speaks of the great shofar which
   will herald the messianic age (Isaiah 27:13).
10. The shofar will be sounded at the resurrection.[3]

The blowing of the shofar is the rallying call of Rosh
Hashanah. Because it is not an easy instrument to master,
a Jewish congregation often goes to great lengths to locate
an accomplished expert, known as a *Ba'al Tekiah*, to
sound the trumpet on Rosh Hashanah.

There are three basic sounds: the *tekiah*, or "blast," is
a short bass note ending abruptly, which symbolizes the
righteous and rejoices in their future when they will receive their reward. The *teruah*, or "trump," is a long, resonant blast, a symbol of awe, which serves to remind how
the wicked quake and tremble in the fear of the day of
judgment; and the *shevarim*, or "quavers," a series of trills
between the other two sounds, representing the average
man, who is filled with joy, sadness, and hope on the feast
of Trumpets.[4]

These shofar blasts are not sounded in an arbitrary
manner; they have been prescribed in detail by centuries
of tradition, and their order may not be modified.

The shofar is also blown during the morning services
of New Year's Day, except on the Sabbath, when blowing of
the shofar is prohibited in modern Judaism. In ancient
times the shofar was sounded on the Sabbath only in the
Temple, not in the synagogues.

3. Sefer Avudarham, *Rosh Hashanah* (Amsterdam, 1726), p. 100; *Encyclopedia Judaica*, vol. 14 (Jerusalem: Keter Publishing House,
1972), p. 309.
4. Isaac ben Moses Arama, cited in Phillip Goodman, *The Rosh Hashanah Anthology* (Philadelphia: Jewish Publication Society of America,
1973), p. 38.

The first blast is heard after the reading of the prophets, while the congregation is seated. A blessing is recited: "Blessed art Thou, O Lord our God, King of the Universe, who has sanctified us by Thy commandments and commanded us to hear the sound of the shofar."

The *Ba'al Tekiah*, the blower of the shofar, covers his head with his prayer shawl and sounds the blasts. In unison, the congregation responds with the verse: "How blessed are the people who know the joyful sound! O Lord, they walk in the light of Thy countenance" (Psalm 89:15).

The sounding of the shofar in the morning service is a solemn time when God is entreated to have mercy on His people: "Israel is the people who knows how to win over their Creator with the blasts of the shofar so that He rises from His throne of judgment to His throne of mercy and is filled with compassion for them and turns His quality of judgment into the quality of compassion" (Leviticus Rabbah 29:4).

THE THREE THEMES OF ROSH HASHANAH

The shofar-sounding ceremony is repeated four more times in the morning service, during the recitation of the "Standing Prayer," or *Amidah*, at which the congregation rises. Each time the blast recalls the three great themes of the holiday: kingship, remembrance, and the sound of the shofar. These themes are depicted in great detail in the *Mahzor*, the special prayer book for the high holy day season. The word *mahzor* literally means "cycle." It is the prayerbook used especially on Rosh Hashanah and Yom Kippur.

As with all Sabbaths and holidays, the morning synagogue service is divided into three parts: a morning prayer (*shaharit*), Scripture reading from the Law and the Prophets, and additional prayer (*musaf*). Many of the special holiday prayers are found in this last, additional section. The *musaf* for Rosh Hashanah reflects the three themes mentioned above.

The rabbis explained these three themes as God saying: "Recite before Me on Rosh Hashanah malhuyot, zihronot and shofarot: Malhuyot so that you may proclaim Me King over you; zihronot so that your remembrance may rise favorably before Me; and through what? Through the shofar" (Rosh Hashanah 16a).

THE BIBLE READINGS

It is appropriate that so many Bible verses are read on this holiday, since the rabbis claim many biblical events occurred on Rosh Hashanah. The sacrifice of Isaac is the most prominent of those, and that is reflected in the portion of the Pentateuch that is read in the synagogue on this day. The synagogue readings on Rosh Hashanah are: Genesis 21 and 1 Samuel 1:1–2:10 on the first day, Genesis 22 and Jeremiah 31:2-20 on the second day, and Numbers 29:1-6 on both days.

The rabbis believe Joseph went forth from prison on New Year's, and on Rosh Hashanah the bondage of their ancestors in Egypt ceased (Rosh Hashanah 10b-11a).

Another event that supposedly occurred on Rosh Hashanah was the birth of Samuel. This is reflected in the holiday's Scripture readings (1 Samuel 1:2-10). Another rabbinical tradition claims that this was the day in which Hannah's prayers were heard by God rather than the day of Samuel's birth.

The idea of motherhood is a central theme of the feast. Sarah and Hannah were each blessed with a child after they seemed destined to be barren. The devotion of those Hebrew mothers to their children has been an inspiration to the Jewish people throughout history. Even the love of God is compared to that of a mother caring for her child:

"As one whom his mother comforts, so will I comfort you" (Isaiah 66:13).

One final Scripture passage read on Rosh Hashanah (Jeremiah 31:2-20) also speaks of a parent's love: "Is Ephraim my dear son? Is he a pleasant child? For as often as I speak against him, I do earnestly remember him still" (v. 20).

<h2 style="text-align:center">CASTING SINS INTO THE DEEP</h2>

Following the afternoon services on Rosh Hashanah comes the ceremony of Tashlich, the symbolic casting of sins into running water. A religious congregation will meet at a river or stream. The rabbis specify that the water should contain fish. Some say that they are a reminder of the eyes of God, which are ever open as are those of a fish.

Here special prayers of repentance are recited: "You will cast all their sins into the depths of the sea, and may You cast all the sins of Your people, the house of Israel, into a place where they shall be no more remembered or visited or ever come to mind."[5]

While the following passage from the book of Micah is read, the people shake crumbs from their pockets into the water. As the crumbs float away, it is supposed that the people's sins, represented by the crumbs, are carried away by the flowing water.

> He will again have compassion upon us; He will tread our iniquities under foot. Yes, Thou wilt cast all their sins into the depths of the sea. Thou wilt give truth to Jacob and unchanging love to Abraham, which Thou didst swear to our forefathers from the days of old. (Micah 7:19-20)

5. Siegel and Strassfeld, p. 122.

The curious ceremony of Tashlich is certainly not biblical, nor is it mentioned in the Talmud. In fact, there is no record of it until the fifteenth century. Since then, its meaning has baffled the sages, as they strive to understand its symbolism. One interpretation is that the sight of water on New Year's Day is intended to remind us that the world was created out of watery chaos. Another view is that the fish in the water remind us that mankind is "like fish caught in a treacherous net" (Ecclesiastes 9:12). Another more interesting story refers to the ancient legend that when Abraham was about to sacrifice Isaac (an event that supposedly occurred on this holiday), Satan set before him a violent stream to stop him. Abraham, undeterred, crossed over the stream and followed the call of God.

Whatever interpretation is preferred, the symbolism of the Tashlich ceremony is obvious. As the Jewish person "casts" his sins into the sea, he hopes and prays that at this time of judgment, God will overlook his failings of the past year.

THE MOOD CHANGES

Though the mood of the synagogue service is solemn, the rabbis say that one should depart the synagogue in a cheerful mood, confident that God has compassionately heard his prayers and the sound of the shofar. As the following rabbinic passage expresses it,

> It is the custom of men who appear before a court of justice to wear black clothes, to let their beards grow long because the outcome is uncertain. But Israel does not do so. On the day of judgment (Rosh Hashanah), they wear white garments and have their beards shaven and they eat, drink, and rejoice in the conviction that God will perform miracles for them. (Rosh Hashanah 1:3, 57b)

The custom of feasting on Rosh Hashanah is based upon the incident in the book of Nehemiah when the people are told, "Go, eat of the fat, drink of the sweet, and send portions to him who has nothing prepared; for this day is holy to our Lord" (Nehemiah 8:10). That passage also explains the Jewish tradition of inviting the needy for Rosh Hashanah meals.

CELEBRATION IN THE HOME

Whereas much of the ritual of Rosh Hashanah takes place in the synagogue, the family table calls forth the real joy of the holiday. The woman of the house begins the celebration by lighting the festival candles ushering in the New Year. Then, rather than going with her family to the synagogue, she stays home to prepare the sumptuous feast that will greet them when they return.

The table is set even more beautifully on Rosh Hashanah than on the Sabbath—the best crystal and china glimmer on lace tablecloths, and polished silver glows in the candlelight. In the center of the table is a colorful arrangement of fruits and honeycake, symbols of the family's hopes for the year ahead. Sweet cakes have traditionally been eaten on Rosh Hashanah, a custom said to be traceable to King David (2 Samuel 6:15, 19).

On this day it is considered bad luck to eat anything sour or bitter, for such food may be an omen of bitter times to come. Neither are nuts eaten on Rosh Hashanah—not because of any inherent qualities of the nut, but because the rabbis deduced that the word *nut* in Hebrew has the same numerical value as *sin* (after the silent vowel *aleph* is dropped). Therefore, nuts must not be eaten lest they remind the Holy One of that unpleasant subject on the day of judgment.

As the family sits down to the feast, the father chants the special blessing for the New Year and dips a slice of apple into a bowl of honey, saying, "May it be Thy will, O Lord our God, to renew unto us a good and sweet year." The apple, aside from being a fruit of the season, symbolizes the Shekinah, the Divine Presence, which is often referred to as an apple orchard in Jewish mystical writings.[6]

On the second night of Rosh Hashanah (for the entire ritual is repeated the next day), a new fruit is usually placed on the table and also dipped in honey. Outside the land of Israel, the second day of Rosh Hashanah is celebrated exactly as the first, except that instead of apples and honey, a new fruit is added, and the ceremony of *tashlich* is not performed.

Besides the fruit and sweet cakes, the attention of the family is captivated by the special bread baked for the holiday. The Sabbath egg bread, *hallah*, is usually a festive, braided loaf. But on the Jewish New Year, it takes on a special identity. On Rosh Hashanah one can see round *hallot*, symbolizing a crown and reminding us of the kingship theme of the holiday and of the desire for a long span of life. The *hallah* may be baked in the shape of a ladder, a reminder of Jacob's dream in which a ladder connected heaven and earth, and of the hope that our link with heaven may once again be established during this season. Sometimes the bread is baked in the form of a bird, a reminder of God's protection as suggested in Isaiah 31:5: "As birds hovering [over their fledglings] so will the Lord of hosts protect Jerusalem."

In some non-European Jewish communities it was customary to eat the head of an animal on Rosh Hashanah. Some say that this was in remembrance of the ram sacrificed by Abraham as a substitute for his son Isaac. Others believed the eating of a head symbolized that one would become a head, a leader, rather than a tail, a follower. In modern practice, the head of a fish is served, and he who

6. *The Kabbalah,* cited in Siegel and Strassfeld, p. 122.

eats it says: "May it be Thy will that we become like a head and not a tail."[7]

THE NEW YEAR AND THE DAY

Fond hopes for a sweet new year again turn the Jewish people to introspection, for the judgment that was to begin on Rosh Hashanah would end ten days later on the Day of Atonement. The common greeting *"L'shanah tovah tika-tevu,"* "May your name be inscribed [in the book of life]," can only become a reality when the balance scales of judgment are noted on the Day of Atonement. Rosh Hashanah carries with it all the excitement and freshness of a New Year and all the anxiety of an unsettled fate before the King of the universe.

7. Goodman, p. 281.

6
Death and the Afterlife

Judaism bases its beliefs about death and the afterlife on the Old Testament Scriptures. The scarcity of those biblical references accounts for the vast array of rabbinic speculation on the subject through the centuries. There has never been, nor is there now, a unified Jewish view of death and the afterlife. That has produced confusion and uncertainty among Jewish people, and it becomes especially acute during the high holiday season.

DEATH

The rabbis view death matter-of-factly—it is the process of passing from this life into the next: "This world is like a vestibule before the World to Come. Prepare thyself in the vestibule, that thou mayest enter into the hall of the palace" (Avot 4:16).

And yet traditions vary on the reason man must die. Some believe that sin is the source of death: "There is no death without sin" (Shabbat 55a), and since "there is not a righteous man on earth . . . who never sins" (Ecclesiastes 7:20), death is inevitable for all. A second-century rabbi saw death as a natural event. He taught that when God finished His work of creation and declared that it was very good (Genesis 1:31), He was including death as a natural part of life and creation.[1]

---

1. "Death," *Encyclopedia Judaica,* vol. 5, pp. 1423-24.

Death, whatever its causes or circumstances, must be
accepted with faith in God's justice. Jewish martyrs have
gone to their deaths reciting Deuteronomy 6:4: "Hear, O
Israel! The Lord our God, the Lord is one!" This attests to
their confidence in the Holy One and loyalty to Judaism at
the time of death. Deuteronomy 6:4 is known as the *Sh'ma,* a
Hebrew word meaning "hear." The *Sh'ma* is recited every
morning and night by religious Jews.

Death is in God's hands, and He takes each person at
His appointed time. These thoughts are reflected in the
Jewish prayerbook, which instructs a Jewish person to re-
cite the following prayer when dying: "Dear God, I want to
live, but if this is Your decree, I accept it from Your hand.
Take care of my loved ones with whom my soul is bound
up; into Your hand I commit my soul. Hear, O Israel, the
Lord our God, the Lord is one."[2]

Those who are approaching death are instructed by
the rabbis to make a final confession. The Mishna says:
"Everyone who makes his confession [before death] has a
share in the world to come" (Sanhedrin 6:2). Some rabbis
even believed that a man's own death could atone for his
sins. That can be seen in the formula for the confession at
the time of death: "O may my death be an atonement for
all the sins, iniquities, and transgressions of which I have
been guilty against Thee."[3] But the rabbis can give little assurance that such "atonement" will give a man peace beyond the grave.

THE AFTERLIFE

According to mainline Judaism, there are two possibi-
lities for the future of a man's soul after death: *immortal-*

2. Jack Riemer, "Jewish Reflections on Death," *Illif Review,* vol. 38, p.
   12.
3. Joseph Hertz, *Authorized Daily Prayer Book* (New York: Bloch,
   1948), p. 1065.

ity, the continued existence of the soul apart from the flesh; or *resurrection*, the eventual reunion of the soul with its original physical body.

IMMORTALITY OF THE SOUL

The teaching that the soul lives on after death, without being once again united with the body in resurrection, is called the "immortality of the soul." In apocryphal literature, Jewish martyrs were promised that their souls would live eternally with God (4 Maccabees 9:8; 17:5, 18). The first-century Jewish philosopher Philo believed the soul was imprisoned in the body and released only at death, either to return to God or suffer eternal death. Today Jewish people affirm the belief in the soul's survival by reciting various prayers in memory of the dead. One of the best known prayers is "May God Remember" (*Yizkor*):

> May God remember the soul of (person) who has gone to his (her) eternal home. I pledge charity in his (her) behalf and on account of this may his (her) soul be bound up in the bond of eternal life among the souls of Abraham, Isaac and Jacob, Sarah, Rebekah, Rachel and Leah, and all the righteous men and women in paradise, Amen.[4]

The Kaddish is also a well-known memorial prayer. Although it does not mention death or dying, it is nevertheless recited in memory of the deceased. (See Hertz, pp. 212, 269-71, 1106-9 for other examples of memorial prayers.)

RESURRECTION

The resurrection of the dead is a prominent theme in Jewish religious thought. It is a basic tenet of Maimonides' "Thirteen Articles of the Faith," one of the few doctrinal

4. "Afterlife," *Encyclopedia Judaica*, vol. 2, p. 339.

statements of the Jewish religion: "I believe with perfect faith that there will be a revival of the dead at the time when it shall please the Creator, blessed be His Name, and exalted be His fame for ever and ever."[5] (Maimonides himself, however, believed in the immortality of the soul [*Guide for the Perplexed* 2:27; 3:54].)

For centuries Jewish people have debated whether or not resurrection is taught in the Hebrew Bible. The Sadducees said no; the Pharisees said yes. Jesus appealed to the Torah when the Sadducees disputed with Him over this matter: "Have you not read that which was spoken to you by God, saying, "I am the God of Abraham, and the God of Isaac, and the God of Jacob? God is not the God of the dead, but of the living" (Matthew 22:31-32). God didn't say, "I was the God of Abraham, Isaac and Jacob," but, "I am the God of Abraham, Isaac and Jacob." The Lord must therefore regard Abraham, Isaac, and Jacob as alive or at least destined to live again.

The question of who will be resurrected is debated. The Mishna declares that "all Israel has a share in the world to come" (Sanhedrin 10:1), except anyone who denies the inspiration of the Torah, and anyone who denies that the resurrection is taught in the Torah (Sanhedrin 10:1; see all of Sanhedrin 10 and Sanhedrin 90b-91a for a list of others who are excluded from the World to Come).

A number of rabbis were also prepared to argue that righteous Gentiles would be included in the World to Come. "Shout joyfully to the Lord all the earth" (Psalm 100:1). Rabbi Jacob in the name of Rabbi Abbahu in the name of Rabbi Aha said: "God said, 'Let all the nations give thanks unto me, and I will receive them.' "[6]

---

5. Cited in Hertz, p. 212.
6. Claude G. Montefiore and Herbert Loewe, *A Rabbinic Anthology* (New York: Schocken, 1974), p. 565; see also Abraham Cohen, *Everyman's Talmud* (New York: Dutton), p. 369.

The belief in the resurrection of the dead is commonly accepted today by religious Jews, who pray in their liturgy: "Blessed art Thou, O Lord, who restorest souls unto the dead,"[7] and, "Blessed art Thou, O Lord, who revivest the dead."[8]

THE MESSIANIC AGE

The messianic age is seen as a political utopia that occurs when the Messiah restores Israel and rules in Jerusalem.[9] The Lord will make the entire earth a paradise, where the climate will be perfect and lavish foods available to all.

THE WORLD TO COME

The conclusion of the messianic age begins an era the rabbis call "the World to Come." At that time, God alone will reign supreme, and the wicked will be punished for their iniquities. While the wicked are punished, the righteous will receive their reward—eternal bliss in the presence of God: "In the World to Come there is no eating nor drinking nor propagation nor business nor jealousy nor hatred nor competition, but the righteous sit with their crowns on their heads feasting on the brightness of the Shekinah" (Berakhot 17a). That forms a fascinating parallel to Paul's statement about the kingdom of God found in Romans 14:17, "For the kingdom of God is not eating and drinking, but righteousness and peace and joy in the Holy Spirit."

One strain of tradition suggests that there will be a period of purgatory, after which the righteous will ascend, and the wicked will descend.[10] But more common is belief

7. Hertz, p. 19.
8. Ibid., p. 135.
9. "Afterlife," *Encyclopedia Judaica,* vol. 2, p. 338.
10. Ibid., p. 337.

in a general resurrection, followed by a judgment in which everyone will give an account of his deeds before God.

GEHINNOM

Those who are deemed unrighteous are sent to Gehinnom, the Jewish word for hell. Gehinnom was a small valley southwest of the old city of Jerusalem where people used to sacrifice their children in the fire to the idol Molech. It was also a place for burning garbage, and one of the only places near Jerusalem where lepers could gather. To the Israelites, this was a fitting symbol of the eternal judgment and contempt that the wicked must endure. In time, Gehinnom came to be regarded as a general place of punishment and not so much a particular valley in Israel. The torment of Gehinnom will go on forever, although some say it will eventually end in some form of annihilation. (For biblical concepts of Gehinnom, see 2 Kings 23:10; 2 Chronicles 28:3; 33:6; Jeremiah 19:2; 32:35; Matthew 5:29; 10:28.)

THE GARDEN OF EDEN

After the judgment, the righteous enter Gan Eden, the Garden of Eden, an actual place on earth. There are stories in rabbinic literature of human travelers coming upon this garden by chance but being driven away by an angel with a flaming sword.[11]

The Talmud eloquently describes Gan Eden and its delights, even speaking of a "marriage" that will take place between God and Israel. The chief joy they will experience is to be in the actual presence of God.

11. Louis Jacobs, *A Guide to Yom Kippur* (London: Jewish Chronicle Pub., 1957), pp. 314-15.

Modern Jewish Thought

Many modern Jews are rationalists and do not believe in an afterlife. The following statement recently issued by the Reform movement reflects this:

> We reassert the doctrine of Judaism, that the soul of man is immortal, grounding this belief on the divine nature of the human spirit, which forever finds bliss in righteousness and misery in wickedness. We reject as ideas not rooted in Judaism the belief both in bodily resurrection and in Gehenna and Eden [hell and paradise], as abodes for eternal punishment or reward.[12]

A popular belief among modern Jews is that the deceased continue to exist in the memories of the living. That does not speak of their immortality as persons, though, but rather the continuation of their influence in the lives of the living.

Conclusion

As we have seen, there is no uniform view on death and the afterlife in Judaism. The sages speculate about the afterlife in parables that speak of the indescribable joy that awaits the righteous and the misery that will be experienced by the wicked, but the details are vague.

Most Jewish people are uncertain about life beyond the grave. Many have no hope or interest in the matter at all. Yet worship on the High Holy Days reminds every Jew of life's fragility—that there exists a higher Authority to whom all must one day answer. At least during this brief time every year the ancient question of Job reverberates, even to this day: "But man dies and lies prostrate. Man expires, and where is he?" (Job 14:10).

12. W. Gunther Plaut, *The Growth of Reform Judaism* (Cincinnati: World Union for Progressive Judaism, 1965), p. 34.

7
The Akedah: The Binding of Isaac

We do not know when Abraham was told to sacrifice his son. In light of that awesome command from God, dates and times seemed inconsequential. Yet Jewish tradition suggests a date: the first of Tishri, or Rosh Hashanah.

Pious Jews plead with God to impute to them the merits of the fathers, especially their most righteous ancestor, Abraham, who was faithful to the point of offering his son as a sacrifice to God. The Jewish people remind God that indeed, there *is* some goodness in man, as if saying, "Look at Abraham, Lord, at what he was willing to sacrifice for You! Surely there must be some degree of his faithfulness in us! Won't you look upon us with mercy for his sake? We cannot measure up to him, but we beg for your mercy on account of his righteousness!"

Abraham is not the only forefather whose merit God is implored to transfer to his people. It is a deep-running strain in Jewish tradition that the merits of the fathers are a storehouse of righteousness from which Jews of every age may draw. For Isaac, Jacob, Joseph, David—all these and many other righteous in Israel are counted as having earned the favor of God. And it is especially at the time of Rosh Hashanah, when the hearts of the people are most sensitive to God's perception of them, that the imputation of these merits is sought.

The following prayer is recited on Rosh Hashanah: "Remember unto us, O Lord our God, the covenant and the lovingkindness and the oath which Thou swore unto Abraham our father on Mount Moriah: and consider the binding with which he suppressed his compassion in order to perform Thy will with a perfect heart. So may Thy compassion overbear Thine anger against us; in Thy great goodness may Thy great wrath turn aside from Thy people, Thy city, and Thine inheritance."

The Akedah, the binding of Isaac, is deeply woven into the fabric of the Jewish consciousness. During the Middle Ages, various hymns of penitence were inspired by the Akedah, and a series of special prayers called "Akedah" have found their way into Jewish liturgy. Religious Jews recite the story daily, and in many prayer books the entire story of the Akedah is printed as part of the early morning service.[1]

ABRAHAM AND GOD THE FATHER

A PROMISE

Following the call of God, Abraham left the comfort of Ur of the Chaldees. God's promise beckoned to him: "And I will make you a great nation . . . and in you all the families of the earth shall be blessed" (Genesis 12:2-3). Yet as the years passed and Abraham saw his earthly strength failing, he began to question God. After a time, he was even beginning to doubt.

"O Lord God," Abraham complained, "what wilt Thou give me, since I am childless, and the heir of my house is Eliezer of Damascus?" (Genesis 15:2). God reiterated His promise of descendants from Abraham's own loins: "This man will not be your heir; but one who shall come forth from your own body, he shall be your heir" (Genesis 15:1).

1. "Akedah," *Encyclopedia Judaica*, vol. 2, p. 481.

In time, God appeared to Abraham at the oaks of Mamre, saying, "I will surely return to you at this time next year; and behold, Sarah your wife shall have a son" (Genesis 18:10).

A MIRACULOUS BIRTH

Abraham was past the time of siring a child, and Sarah, his wife, had been barren all her life. There was no earthly reason to expect that God would fulfill His promise. Yet Abraham believed God, and it was imputed to him as righteousness (Genesis 15:6; Romans 4:3).

God *did* fulfill His promise, and from Abraham and Sarah's union, He wrought the miraculous. God, who closed the wombs of Abimelech's household (Genesis 20:18), gave Sarah a child (Genesis 21:2). Though she was "beyond the proper time of life," and Abraham was "as good as dead," Isaac was born (Hebrews 11:12).

THE WILLINGNESS OF ABRAHAM

We cannot possibly fathom the love that Abraham felt for Isaac. Yet as great as his love was for his son, Abraham's love for God was even greater, for at God's request he was willing to sacrifice his soul's delight upon the altar. In Isaac was the culmination of God's promises. For Isaac he had left Ur. For Isaac he lived a life of wandering. Isaac was the fruit of Abraham's self-sacrificing life. God speaks of Isaac as Abraham's "only son" (Genesis 22:16), ignoring Ishmael, who was not the child of promise.

Great indeed was Abraham's love for Isaac, yet it pales when compared with God's love for His own Son. Abraham's love had grown from a close, intimate fellowship throughout the child's life, but the fellowship of the Father and the Son existed from eternity! Abraham's love was temporal, but the Father's love for Jesus was eternal.

And God did not ask of Abraham what He would ultimately demand from Himself. He did not allow Abraham to slay His son, yet He did not spare His own Son. He was obligated by His holiness to turn His face from the One He had loved through all eternity. In this the love of God was perfectly expressed; He allowed His only Son to die for the sins of unworthy men (Romans 5:8). Abraham's love for Isaac and his willingness to sacrifice his son are only the dimmest foreshadowing of God's own sacrifice on behalf of the world.

ISAAC—A FORESHADOWING OF CHRIST

Like Isaac's birth, the birth of Jesus was a miracle. The child Jesus was conceived through the power of the Holy Spirit (Luke 1:35).

In the same way He made a promise to Abraham, God promised to send His Son to be the redeemer of Abraham's seed and of the whole world. Centuries before His birth, the Scriptures foretold the coming of One who would be God incarnate. His miraculous birth would bring the Lord Himself to dwell among men (Isaiah 7:14). He would be worthy to bear the name of God (Isaiah 9:6-7) and receive the homage of the nations (Psalm 2). Proverbs also contains an astounding reference to Him: "Who has ascended into heaven and descended? Who has gathered the wind in His fists? Who has wrapped the waters in His garment? Who has established all the ends of the earth? What is His name or His Son's name? Surely you know!" (Proverbs 30:4).

Isaac was certainly a type of the greater Son whose coming would fulfill the hopes of all people. Yet Isaac was more than merely a type, for it was from his own loins that the future Son of Promise would be born. Jesus the Messiah was a direct descendant of Isaac.

The promised son of Abraham leads us to the promised Son of God in whom all is fulfilled—the promises to Abraham, Isaac, Moses, David, Israel, and all the world.

HIS INNOCENCE

We do not know Isaac's age at the time of the Akedah. We assume he was a youth, but some rabbis suggest that he may have been thirty-seven years old (Genesis Rabbah 56:8). He was definitely old enough to carry the wood for the burnt offering to Mount Moriah. He may have been of age to sin, but certainly he was not guilty of any crime deserving death.

Jesus is portrayed by Scripture as perfectly innocent and without sin: "He had done no violence, nor was there any deceit in His mouth" (Isaiah 53:9b). He died for the sins of the ungodly who deserved the penalty instead (Isaiah 53:6). Like the substitute ram God provided for Isaac, Jesus was the perfect substitute for us. And we can rejoice with Abraham that God has "provided for Himself the lamb for the burnt offering" (Genesis 22:8). Jesus is the Lamb of God.

HIS OBEDIENCE

Isaac accompanied Abraham, never expecting that he himself was to be the burnt offering. When he questioned his father about the sacrificial lamb, he was readily assured by Abraham that God would provide the animal at the right time.

Isaac must have been terrified as his father took the rope, wound it around him, and placed his bound body upon the altar. Yet he lay without struggle. In obedience to his beloved father and to God, Isaac allowed himself to be prepared for sacrifice.

Abraham stretched out his arm, gathering the courage to plunge the blade into his son's flesh. Suddenly, he heard a voice. "Abraham! . . . do not stretch out your hand against the lad . . . for now I know that you fear God, since you have not withheld your son, your only son, from Me" (Genesis 22:11-12).

Abraham's thankfulness to discover the substitute ram was beyond description. But what of Isaac's feelings? Was he not justified in resenting the God who had demanded his life for no apparent reason? No! Throughout the rest of his life, Isaac continued to be an obedient son and a faithful follower of his father's God. What an example of faith and obedience!

The obedience of Jesus was much greater still. In agony, He cried out to God to be delivered from the bitter cup of death, yet obedience to His Father's will propelled Him to His destiny, to fulfill the mission for which He had come. Hundreds of years before, the prophet Isaiah had written, "He was oppressed and He was afflicted, yet He did not open His mouth; like a lamb that is led to slaughter, and like a sheep that is silent before its shearers, so He did not open His mouth" (Isaiah 53:7).

The New Testament confirms Jesus' obedience to His Father. For even though He was the Son of God, "He learned obedience from the things which He suffered" (Hebrews 5:8).

HIS DEATH AND RESURRECTION

The Scripture recounts Abraham's willingness to sacrifice Isaac as he held the knife poised. Yet God stayed his hand, and Isaac's life was spared. In Abraham's heart, however, the sacrifice had been made, and that was sufficient in the eyes of God.

The rabbis believed that the sacrifice of Isaac was more than a "close call." One passage of the traditional literature tells us that Isaac actually died of terror while bound upon the altar and was revived by the voice from heaven telling his father to stay the knife (Pirke de Rabbi Eliezer 31). In this view, Isaac's death was an accomplished fact, and his life from that point became a resurrection life. A variation of that tradition tells us that Isaac was burned to ashes upon the altar but then was resurrected to new life.[2] The belief that Isaac was resurrected and that his death brought atonement and forgiveness to Israel is held by a minority of rabbis (Canticles Rabbah 1:14).

The Mekhilta[3] identifies the blood of the Passover lamb with the blood of Isaac,[4] and in another work the daily morning and evening sacrifices in the Temple were spoken of as memorials of the offering of Isaac (Leviticus Rabbah 2).

The same idea is found in an ancient paraphrase of Leviticus 22:27, "The lamb was chosen [as the sacrificial animal] to recall the merit of the lamb of Abraham who bound himself upon the altar and stretched out his neck for the sake of Thy name."[5]

The Jewish writers of the New Testament echoed this traditional belief, as they spoke of Isaac as a type of Christ. The author of Hebrews wrote, "He [Abraham] considered that God is able to raise men even from the dead; from which he also received him back as a type" (Hebrews 11:19). Whether or not Isaac actually died and was resurrected, he *was* offered to God in Abraham's heart and returned to his father as if raised from the dead.

2. Rosenberg, p. 387.
3. *Mekhilta* is an Aramaic word meaning "a measure." The Mekhilta is a collection of rabbinic legal exegesis on the book of Exodus. There are two works: the Mekhilta of Rabbi Ishmael and the Mekhilta of Rabbi Simeon ben Yohai. Technically, the Mekhilta is a form of Midrash (*Encyclopedia Judaica,* vol. 11, pp. 1267-68).
4. Mekhilta 8a, ed. Lauterbach, tractate Piska, chap. 7, p. 57.
5. Rosenberg, p. 388.

THE HOPE OF RESURRECTION

God offered His Son on Calvary's altar knowing that Jesus would rise from the dead. That, however, did not diminish the torment of His sacrifice, for Jesus still had to endure the indescribable pain of death.

Abraham believed God could raise Isaac from the dead. When he told his servants that he and Isaac were going up to the mountain to offer the sacrifice, he said, "Stay here with the donkey, and I and the lad will go yonder; and we will worship and return to you" (Genesis 22:5). Abraham did not say, "If we return." He said, "We *will* return." He had faith that the lad would come back.

Resurrection hope must have been central to Abraham's faith. How else could he resolve the conflict between God's command to sacrifice his son and the divine promise that was rooted in Isaac? By slaying his son he was not only slaying the desire of his heart but seemingly frustrating the promise of God. His hope in the resurrection enabled him to obey God, even when it seemed that all would be destroyed.

THE MESSAGE OF SUBSTITUTIONARY SACRIFICE

Some have ventured to say that God instituted the practice of substitutionary sacrifice when He made clothing for Adam and Eve to cover their nakedness. But the sacrifice of Isaac is the first clear instance of substitutionary death in redemption's history. Isaac was required to die on that altar, yet God Himself provided a substitute, a ram caught by its horns in the thicket. The Scripture then states that Abraham "offered him [the ram] up for a burnt offering *in the place* of his son" (italics added).

The "life-for-life" principle of substitutionary sacrifice is established. Some rabbis say that by providing the ram in Isaac's place, God was condemning all human sacrifice.

However, the foundational principle of the divine sacrificial system, that one life may atone for another, is initiated here by God Himself.

It is especially significant, then, that the offering of Isaac took place on Mount Moriah. The name *Moriah* is composed of two words, one meaning "to see" and the other being the name of God. The name literally means "the shown of Jehovah" or even "the manifestation of Jehovah." Abraham called the mountain "Jehovah Jireh," which means "God will provide." Little did he know that the same mountain would provide substitution for multitudes of his descendants. Mount Moriah would be the site of God's Holy Temple—the one place on the earth where acceptable sacrifices could be offered and where His Shekinah presence would dwell. The binding of Isaac prefigures the entire sacrificial system as ultimately fulfilled in Jesus Christ.

THE FOREBEARER OF THE FAITHFUL

Isaac, the "child of promise," lived as having been resurrected from the dead. In this, he is a type of all New Covenant believers, for we too live in "newness of life," having died with Christ and been made alive through His resurrection (Romans 6:4). As Paul writes in Galatians 4:28, "And you brethren, like Isaac, are children of promise."

In *The Gospel in the Feasts of Israel*, Victor Buksbazen summarized the relationship between the Akedah and the New Testament believer, between Abraham and God the Father, and between Isaac and Christ. He wrote, "Abraham's sacrifice of Isaac typified gloriously the sacrifice of our Heavenly Father of His Son, the Lord Jesus Christ, and

6. *New American Standard Bible* notes, p. 19; Frederic Keil and Franz Delitzsch, *Old Testament Commentaries*, vol. 1, reprint (Grand Rapids: Associated Publishers and Authors, n.d.), p. 193.

the willingness of the Son to offer Himself unto salvation of all men. Isaac is a beautiful type of Christ."[7]

The Akedah, so important in Jewish religious thought and life, must be given new consideration by those who cherish this same resurrection hope. One day the shofar will blow, and the spiritual descendants of Isaac will be raised to meet the greater Son of Isaac and enjoy His presence forever. Until then, may the willingness of Abraham and the obedience of Isaac serve as inspiring examples.

7. Buksbazen, p. 26.

Part 2:

Yom Kippur

8

The Biblical Institution
of Yom Kippur

Man's sin has separated him from God. Yet the Lord thought it of ultimate importance to restore that relationship. He ordained the single most important day of the Jewish year as the Day of Atonement.

The theme of holiness is central to the Day of Atonement, as it is to the entire book of Leviticus. The Hebrew word for holy, *kadosh,* is used more than eighty times. The message of the third book of the Torah is found in these verses, "Speak to all the congregation of the sons of Israel and say to them, 'You shall be holy, for I the Lord your God am holy' " (Leviticus 19:2), and, "Thus you are to be holy to me, for I the Lord am holy; and I have set you apart from the peoples to be Mine" (Leviticus 20:26).

God desired Israel to live sanctified lives and gave the Mosaic law to instruct His people in holy living. The word *holy* comes from the Hebrew word *kadosh* meaning "to set apart" or "to cut apart." Like their Creator, Israel was to be separated from sin and from the heathen influence of the nations of the world. The Scripture speaks of two types of sin—sin of commission (committing an unlawful act) and sin of omission (failing to obey God's decree). Israel was charged by God to abhor both.

Although the laws of Leviticus were given to instruct the people in holiness, the principle of grace flows deeply through the book. God realized that Israel could never maintain His perfect standards. So in His grace He provided the sacrificial system, a way for Israel to be once again reconciled to God in covenant fellowship.

The sacrificial system and especially the Day of Atonement are an expression of God's compassion and grace. Too often the Mosaic law is viewed as a harsh taskmaster, even when the New Testament affirms that the law is good (Romans 7:12). The law of Moses is a series of instructions given to help Israel live holy lives. And within the core of the Mosaic law is sacrifice, evidence that God knew Israel would not be able to keep the law. The sacrificial system declares God's grace and His willingness to forgive the sins of His people.

Thus He set aside an entire day to make atonement for their souls, one gracious day each year when every individual could find forgiveness for past sins and be restored to fellowship with his Maker.

The Old Testament system of animal sacrifices has not usually been portrayed as an expression of God's grace and mercy. The apostle John wrote, "For the Law was given through Moses; grace and truth were realized through Jesus Christ" (John 1:17). Some have interpreted this passage to mean that grace was nonexistent in the Old Covenant. Yet this verse merely teaches that the grace and truth expressed in the Old Testament were fully realized when God, who is all grace and all truth, became incarnate and dwelt among men. Jesus Christ is God's living example of the grace and truth foreshadowed in the Old Testament Scriptures. God's grace is demonstrated many times in the Hebrew Scriptures.

The benefits of the Day of Atonement were short lived, though. It is wrong to assume that the atonement wrought by Yom Kippur had value for the following year. It did not.

The atonement was effective only as long as an Israelite remained perfectly and completely obedient to the law, and that could not have been for long. The Yom Kippur sacrifices needed to be repeated annually.

The Day of Atonement foreshadowed the great day when salvation and atonement would be made for Israel and the Gentiles through the death of God's Son at Calvary.

THE NAME: DAY OF ATONEMENT

The biblical name for the Day of Atonement is *Yom Hakippurim,* meaning "the day of covering or concealing." The holiday has been called by different names throughout the centuries. Occasionally, it was called "The Day of the Fast" or "The Great Fast." In the Talmud the name was shortened to simply "The Day." The Aramaic version of this name, "Yoma," was given to the Talmudic tractate describing in detail the rituals of the day. Philo called the tenth of Tishri "The Fast" (*Treatise on the Ten Festivals,* the Ninth Festival), and Josephus merely speaks of it as the tenth day of the same lunar month, without giving it any name (*Antiquities* 3.10). When describing Pompey's invasion of Jerusalem in 63 B.C., though, Josephus does call the holiday "The Day of the Fast." In Acts, Luke makes reference to Yom Kippur, which he calls "The Fast."

The sacrificial system was designed to cover sin until it was finally put away through the death of Christ. Atonement hides rather than removes sin from God's sight. The covering is total and allows God to look upon the Israelites as if their sin did not exist. God creates a shelter of sacrificial blood to protect worshipers from His wrath.

One more facet to atonement is illustrated by a related word, *kopher,* which means a ransom of money. In Exodus 21:30 the law allows that a monetary ransom be paid for an individual deserving death. The guilty party here was the owner of an ox that had previously gored a man to death and then did so to a second person. Exodus 21:29 tells us that the owner of the ox should be put to death unless he offered a suitable ransom for his own life. "If a ransom is demanded of him, then he shall give for the redemption [*koper*] of his life whatever is demanded of him" (Exodus 21:30). This ransom is a substitute enabling the guilty party to remain alive.

Another passage (Exodus 30:12) instructs every Israelite to give the ransom money of half a shekel to the service of the sanctuary. But in the case of a murder, no ransom could be given in exchange for that individual's life (Numbers 35:31).

God told the Israelite to sacrifice an animal as a substitute for his own sentence of death. This "life for life" principle is the foundation of the sacrificial system. As each animal met its gory end, Jewish worshipers would graphically be reminded of sin's ugly price. The Lord said: "For the life of the flesh is in the blood, and I have given it to you on the altar to make atonement for your souls; for it is the blood by reason of the life that makes atonement" (Leviticus 17:11).

Blood was a symbol of life. Moishe Rosen, commenting on the significance of the blood, writes:

> Blood represents life itself. Blood is a living fluid. It brings nourishment to the body and cleanses wastes. In Leviticus 17:11 God was not saying that he had created blood for the purpose of making an atonement, but that because of its unique, vital biological function he had set it apart and reserved it solely and expressly for that purpose. The Israelites were not to touch it, nor use it for ordinary purposes. In a sense, it was to be regarded as holy.[1]

1. Moishe Rosen, "Blood Sacrifice," *The Jews for Jesus Newsletter* 11:5746, p. 1.

Rosen cites several different uses of blood in the Scripture. The blood:

- is a token of the New Covenant (Matthew 26:28, Luke 22:20, 1 Corinthians 11:25).
- gives life (John 6:54).
- brings redemption (Ephesians 1:7).
- makes propitiation (Romans 3:25).
- justifies (Romans 5:9).
- provides access through forgiveness (Colossians 1:14, Ephesians 1:7, 1 John 1:9, Ephesians 2:13).
- provides reconciliation (Colossians 1:19-20).
- provides cleansing (1 John 1:7).
- makes us overcomers (Revelation 12:11).[2]

THE DATE OF YOM KIPPUR

God ordained that the Day of Atonement should fall on the tenth of Tishri, ten days following the holiday of repentance, the feast of Trumpets. It is significant that repentance must precede redemption. For on Yom Kippur the Israelite was able to act on his repentance by offering a sacrifice for his sins. Animal sacrifices were *only effective* when presented with a contrite and repentant heart (Psalm 51:16-19)

The Day of Atonement was to be celebrated by the Israelites for one day, but that one day was to be kept according to the Scripture as a "perpetual statute." It was to be observed "throughout your generations in all your dwelling places" (Leviticus 23:31).

The word *perpetual,* or as the King James version translates it, "a statute forever," is in itself a limited period of time. The Hebrews thought in terms of ages having a beginning and an end, whereas the Greeks thought in terms of endless time. In the New Testament, the concept of "for-

2. Ibid., pp. 2-3.

ever" is usually expressed by the phrase *aions ton aionon*, the ages of ages.

But the Israelites had no such concept. So each holiday initiated by God has its fulfillment in history. Yom Kippur, the Day of Atonement, was to be celebrated until the day came when a new age of forgiveness dawned and the old age was complete and passed away. That happened with the coming of Christ who made atonement once and for all, and with His resurrection began the age of the New Covenant prophesied in Jeremiah 31:31-34.

It is also noteworthy that God placed Yom Kippur before the feast of Tabernacles, the season of joy. The children of Israel could only rejoice once they were redeemed and their sins forgiven.

The Day of Atonement rises as a peak among the mountains of Israel's feasts—a peak that one must scale to experience true joy. For God could pour out His blessings of joy only upon a forgiven people; when Israel did not observe Yom Kippur, He was forced to dole out judgment.

THE FOUR ELEMENTS OF YOM KIPPUR

Four main elements composed the biblical institution of the Day of Atonement: "On exactly the tenth day of this seventh month is the day of atonement; it shall be *a holy convocation* for you, and you shall *humble your souls* and present an *offering by fire* to the Lord. *Neither shall you do any work* on this same day" (Leviticus 23:27-28, italics added).

HOLD A CONVOCATION

The Day of Atonement was a worship-event, drawing the focus of the Jewish people to the altar of divine mercy. The Holy One called the people of Israel to gather in His presence and give their undivided attention exclusively to Him. All work, even food preparation, was prohibited.

HUMBLE YOUR SOULS

The Scriptures do not elaborate how the people of Israel were to "afflict their souls" (KJV*). The prophet Isaiah, however, seems to parallel the humbling of a soul with fasting (Isaiah 58:3). That theme was expanded by rabbinic writers, who speak of fasting and contrition as a requirement on Yom Kippur. "To afflict [bow, humble] the soul" by restraining the earthly appetites, which have their seat in the soul, is the early Mosaic expression for fasting (*tsum*). The latter word first came into use in the time of the judges (Judges 20:26; 1 Samuel 7:6; Psalm 35:13).[3]

Regardless of how they fulfilled the command, Israel understood that on this day they were to repent and mourn over their sins. The seriousness of the command is evident when God says, "If there is any person who will not humble himself on this same day, he shall be cut off from his people" (Leviticus 23:29).

PRESENT AN OFFERING

The offerings are central to the Day of Atonement ritual. The Bible devotes an entire chapter, Leviticus 16, to them. The offerings are also listed in Numbers 29:7-11. It is through these sacrifices that Israel makes peace with God.

DO NOT WORK

The Day of Atonement is a sabbath of sabbaths (Leviticus 23:32). The Israelites were forbidden to do any work at all (Leviticus 23:31) and were liable to capital punishment if they disobeyed.

* King James Version.
3. Keil and Delitzsch, vol. 1, p. 689.

LEVITICUS 16

GOD MEETS THE HIGH PRIEST

Rather than begin with the Day of Atonement, Leviticus 16 first recounts the death of the two sons of Aaron (Leviticus 10:1-5) who were punished for offering "strange fire" before the Lord. This was more than a mere chronological link or the setting of a historical context. It was a graphic reminder that God's instruction in worship *must* be followed (Leviticus 10:3).

Aaron was warned not to set foot into the Holy of Holies at any other time. God said to Moses: "Tell your brother Aaron that he shall not enter at any time into the holy place inside the veil, before the mercy seat which is on the ark, lest he die; for I will appear in the cloud over the mercy seat" (Leviticus 16:2).

The Lord had issued a solemn warning that no man may see His face and live (Exodus 33:20). But on the Day of Atonement, and only on that day, God made an exception. On Yom Kippur, the high priest was commanded to enter into the presence of the Shekinah in the Holy of Holies and make atonement for the sins of Israel.

When the high priest entered the Holy of Holies, he saw the Lord's presence as a brilliant cloud hovering above the Mercy Seat. The word for Mercy Seat can also be translated "the seat of atonement," for it is the same root, *kafar*, that is used in the Hebrew. The Mercy Seat stood upon the Ark of the Covenant but was not actually a part of it (Exodus 35:12). This place of atonement is described in detail in Exodus 25:17-22 and 37:6-9. It was surrounded by the cherubim who stood as guardians of the divine Presence. The Mercy Seat was so identified with the Holy of Holies that in 1 Chronicles 28:11, the Holy of Holies is referred to as "the room of the mercy seat." And perhaps the Mercy Seat was the most important part of the Holy of Holies, be-

cause it was over the Mercy Seat that the presence of God
dwelt in the cloud.[4]

This was the place in the Tabernacle where Moses met
and spoke with God face to face (Exodus 25:22, 30:6;
Numbers 7:89), where atonement was to be made for the
sins of Israel. It was on this precise location that heaven
reached down to earth, enabling man to make peace with
God.

THE WASHING AND GARMENTS OF THE PRIEST

To enter the Holy of Holies, the high priest was first to
bathe his entire body, going beyond the mere washing of
hands and feet as required for other occasions. The high
priest had to be personally pure if his intercession was to
be accepted. The washings symbolized his desire for purification.

The priest's clothing was designed to reflect the holiness and purity desired by God.

Rather than donning his usual robe and colorful garments (described in Exodus 28 and Leviticus 8), Aaron was
commanded to wear special garments of linen, the same
fabric worn by the angels of the Lord (Ezekiel 9:2-3, 11;
10:2, 6-7; Daniel 10:5; 12:6-7) and by the risen Messiah
Himself (Revelation 1:13-15). The phrase "these are holy
garments" (Leviticus 16:4) is intended to punctuate the
holiness of the occasion.[5] It should especially be noted that
the high priest was not required to wear the Urim and
Thummim on the Day of Atonement. There was no need
for those vestments, which were God's instruments of direct communication to the people, for on this day the high
priest met God face to face.

4. Roland De Vaux, *Ancient Israel: Its Life and Institutions*, trans. John
     McHugh (London: Darton, Longman & Todd, 1973), p. 300.
5. Keil and Delitzsch, vol. 1, p. 682.

THE OFFERINGS OF THE DAY

The Yom Kippur offerings, although not as numerous as those presented during the feast of Tabernacles, brought the sacrificial system to majestic new heights. The offerings on the feast of Tabernacles were expressions of thanksgiving, but on Yom Kippur the Mercy Seat was smeared with blood, making atonement for Israel.

It appears from Numbers 29:7-11 that the offerings for the Day of Atonement are divided into three groups: continual burnt offerings, festive sacrifices, and those sacrifices designed for the Day of Atonement. The continual burnt offerings included the usual sacrifices that were offered in the Temple twice a day. The festive sacrifices were offered for the high priest and the priesthood (a ram for a burnt offering) and for the people of the congregation as well. There were actually two types of sacrifices offered for the people of the congregation: a burnt offering (one young bullock, one ram, and seven lambs of the first year along with their meat offerings) and the sin offering (one kid). The third group of offerings, those especially unique to the Day of Atonement, included a young bullock as a sin offering for the high priest, his household, and the sons of Aaron, and another sin offering for the people of the congregation. The latter consisted of two goats, one of which was killed and its blood sprinkled on the altar and the other sent into the wilderness bearing the iniquities of the children of Israel.[6]

On the first Day of Atonement, Aaron was charged by God to enter the Holy of Holies. Aaron was accustomed to having his brother, Moses, speak to the Lord. Appearing personally before God, though, was new and must have been terrifying for him; perhaps he feared a similar fate as

6. Edersheim, p. 306.

that suffered by his two sons. Would *he* be struck down in the presence of the Shekinah? Aaron had often witnessed God's judgment on those who rebelled against Him.

A great responsibility fell upon Aaron's shoulders. If he did not perfectly execute the intricate Yom Kippur sacrificial ritual, he would subject the people of Israel to God's fiery wrath.

Aaron was commanded to take two handfuls of incense and place them in a fire pan full of coals taken from the altar of God. The cloud arising from that incense would cover the Mercy Seat with the sweet fragrance of Aaron's prayers for forgiveness. Only then was he ready to present the sin offering for himself and his household (Leviticus 16:6, 11).

The glory of God shone brilliantly, enshrouded by the clouds of incense. Aaron, in fear and trembling, took the blood of the bull and sprinkled it on the Mercy Seat, first on the east side, then on the front, seven times. With that offering completed and his own sins atoned for, Aaron was ready to present the sacrifices for the nation.

Two male goats had been selected, and Aaron had cast lots, choosing one to be offered before the Lord and the other as the scapegoat. Aaron slaughtered the first goat on the altar (Leviticus 16:5) and sprinkled the Mercy Seat with its blood (Leviticus 16:15), trusting that God would accept the sacrifice as an atonement for the people of Israel.

Aaron was also charged with making atonement for the Holy of Holies, the tent of meeting, and the altar that stood in the great court (Leviticus 16:16-18, 33). They had become filthy with the sins of the people (Leviticus 16:16). Washing the altar with water could never suffice; only the blood of the Yom Kippur sacrifice would avail, for the blood had the power to restore even the most sacred item to purity. Once the altar, the tent of meeting, and the Holy of Holies were cleansed, they were again fit to be used in divine service.

THE SCAPEGOAT

The high point and most unusual element of the Yom Kippur sacrificial ritual was the ceremony involving the second goat, the scapegoat. Moses wrote:

> Then Aaron shall lay both of his hands on the head of the live goat and confess over it all the iniquities of the sons of Israel and all their transgressions in regard to all their sins; and he shall lay them on the head of the goat and send it away into the wilderness by the hand of a man who stands in readiness. And the goat shall bear on itself all their iniquities to a solitary land; and he shall release the goat in the wilderness. (Leviticus 16:21-22)

The Hebrew word for scapegoat is *azazel*. Other than the four times it is used in this chapter, the word does not appear in the Hebrew Scriptures. Both Jewish and Christian scholars have debated on the meaning of the azazel. Some believe it was simply the name of the goat, others that azazel was the name of the wilderness where the goat was sent to die.

Another school of thought, including that of E. W. Hengstenburg and Keil and Delitzsch, suggested that azazel was the chief of the evil spirits, a synonym for Satan. The goat was sent into the wilderness to take Israel's sins, which God had forgiven, back to Azazel, the father of all sin. Azazel was not an offering to Satan but rather a living demonstration that God had forgiven His people and sent their sins back to their source.[7] The intertestamental book of Enoch (8:1) most clearly associated azazel with the chief of demons and Satan himself. The word *azazel,* however, is never used in reference to a demon in the Scriptures, and

7. Keil and Delitzsch, vol. 1, p. 688.

there do not seem to be biblical or linguistic grounds to accept any of these views.[8]

The root of the word *azazel* contains the idea of removal. The name azazel and the action of sending away the goat was designed to teach the Israelites that their sins, once removed, would also be forgotten. The Septuagint, Vulgate, and a number of other ancient translations understood azazel to literally mean "the goat that departs." The word is viewed as a combination of 'ez, meaning goat, and azal, to turn off or away. Brown, Driver, and Briggs link the word to an Arabic term azala, which means "to banish" or "remove."[9]

A parallel to the azazel is the ceremony of cleansing a cured leper. Two birds were chosen, one to be killed and the other to be dipped in its blood. The live bird was then released, symbolizing to all that the curse of leprosy was totally removed from its former victim (Leviticus 14:1-9). The birds were considered one offering, teaching the lessons of cleansing by blood and removal of the affliction.

Similarly, the two goats were viewed as *one* offering: "And he shall take from the congregation of the sons of Israel two male goats for a sin offering" (Leviticus 16:5, italics added). The slaughtered goat showed the congregation that God's wrath was appeased, while the live goat was sent into the wilderness bearing the sins of Israel, illustrating that they had been removed (Psalm 103:12). This "scapegoat" was just as much a sin offering as the goat that was slaughtered. Keil and Delitzsch write, "The sins, which were thus laid upon its head by confession, were the sins of

8. *Theological Wordbook of the Old Testament*, vol. 1, R. Laird Harris, Gleason Archer, and Bruce Waltke, eds. (Chicago: Moody, 1980), p. 1594.
9. *A Hebrew and English Lexicon of the Old Testament*, ed. Francis Brown, trans. Edward Robinson (Oxford: Clarendon Press, 1st ed. 1907, reprinted with corrections 1972), p. 786.

Israel, which had already been expiated by the sacrifice of the other goat."[10]

The two goats foreshadowed the sacrifice of Christ. When the Messiah died on Calvary, He paid the penalty for our sins, as did the goat that was slaughtered. He also removed sin. But where does the New Testament teach that our sins are *removed* through His sacrifice?

John the Baptist combined the idea of the azazel with the Passover Lamb. Standing on the stones of the Jordan river, John cried: "Behold the Lamb of God who *takes away* the sin of the world" (John 1:29). Jesus is not only the slain Lamb who protects us from the wrath of God (Exodus 12), He is not merely a "sheep led silently to the slaughter" (Isaiah 53), He is also the azazel (Leviticus 16). For through His death, the sins of all who believe are completely removed.

10. Keil and Delitzch, vol. 1, p. 687.

9

Yom Kippur in the Time of Christ

In Christ's day, everything stopped on the Day of Atonement. The Middle Eastern bazaars, usually teeming with enthusiastic shoppers, were empty. Jewish merchants who carried their wares from town to town along fine Roman roads were gone. The day of all days had arrived. Jewish people everywhere gave themselves to the worship of the Holy One who held their temporal and eternal future in His grasp.

Hundreds of synagogues in the Diaspora were filled to capacity for the special holiday services. Tearful confessions were made, the Torah was read, prayers were recited, yet the heart of every Jewish person was turned towards Jerusalem. For on Yom Kippur the destiny of every Jew was decided at the Temple altar, where sacrifices were offered and atonement made for the forgiveness of their sins.

THE TEMPLE

The Temple was a magnificent structure at the time of Christ, admired as one of the wonders of the world. It had recently undergone extensive refurbishing at the hands of Herod. The Talmud, which usually looked unfavorably upon Herod, states: "He who has not seen the Temple of Herod has never in his life seen a beautiful structure" (Baba Bathra 4a). The magnificence of Herod's Temple is acclaimed in the New Testament as well, when one of the disciples said to Jesus,

"Teacher, behold what wonderful stones and what wonderful buildings!" (Mark 13:1). The second Temple was most certainly one of the great wonders of the ancient world. Enlargements and beautifications continued to be made to the structure until A.D. 62, just a few years before its destruction. According to Josephus, the work ended under the procurator Albinus sometime between A.D. 62 and 64. Josephus mentions that when the work was concluded eighteen thousand laborers were left unemployed (*Antiquities* 15.380-402; 20.219).

This "Herodian" Temple was more than twice the size of and far more beautiful than the earlier one built by Ezra and the faithful remnant from Babylon. During Christ's day the Temple area served the Israelites as a public gathering place and a forum where itinerant rabbis could teach. On its premises were a synagogue, various administrative offices, and even areas especially assigned to the vendors of sacrificial animals. Many Jewish people, including Jesus, were indignant over the commercialization of the holy site.

The heart of the Temple was the central structure, which housed the holy place, and the revered Holy of Holies. Into that dark chamber no one would dare enter except the high priest himself, and only on the Day of Atonement, lest the wrath of God strike him dead.

Outside the Holy of Holies was a windowless antechamber, the holy place, containing the golden candelabra, the table of the showbread, and a golden altar on which incense was burned twice a day.

Immediately outside the holy place was the Court of the Priests, which held the Temple treasuries, the meeting place for the Sanhedrin, and special quarters where the high priest lived in preparation for the Day of Atonement. At the front of this structure, for all Israel to see, was a great altar of uncut stones where the eternal fire burned. To the right of the altar was the area where animals were slaughtered, having large marble tables for the carcasses and the utensils used in their sacrifice. Two more courts, the Court of the Levites and the Court of the Israelites, were also within this sacred area.

Just outside the Court of the Israelites, and separated from it by the magnificent Nicanor Gate, was the Court of the Women. Men were allowed to enter the Court of the Israelites, but under no circumstances could a woman approach it. Tall balconies were constructed from which pious women could view the Temple service.

Beyond the Court of the Women, and surrounding the entire Temple complex, was the Court of the Gentiles. Over this court stood an ominous image: a golden Roman eagle, representing the rule of Rome over the Jewish people and casting its shadow over the entire Temple mount. In the Court of the Gentiles, pious non-Jews could come and worship the God of Israel. That was as close as they could get, though, to the holy portions of the Temple, for stern signs were posted upon every gate forbidding Gentiles to pass beyond their court under penalty of death.

Surrounding the Court of the Gentiles was an outer area of magnificent colonnades: Solomon's portico and the Regal Colonnade were the greatest of them, the latter having 162 marble pillars. The colonnades served as a gathering place for the people and were a popular gathering point for the early Jewish Christians. The Sanhedrin often met on the Temple mount as did those purchasing animals for sacrificial use.

The entire complex was built on the same spot as the original Temple of Solomon. Even though it was the third Temple to stand in that place, it was called the "second" Temple, since the previous site had not been destroyed but merely expanded to make way for this one.

Because the Jewish people were so widely dispersed at the time of the second Temple, an elaborate system had developed to ensure that all Israelites would be adequately represented at the Temple service. The territories of Israel and the Diaspora were divided into twenty-four sections, each of which sent two representatives to officiate at the Temple for two weeks of each year.

Worship in Herod's Temple was conducted by twenty-four divisions of Levitical priests. The priests would live in their own homes until their period of service in the Temple. During their ministry in Jerusalem they slept within the Temple precincts. The various Temple duties were divided among them. According to tradition, more than five hundred priests were employed on the Day of Atonement in order to assist the high priest.[1]

Participation in ritual sacrifice was aided by common Israelite representatives divided into what were called "deputations" and based upon the geographical constitution of the twenty-four districts. In Talmudic literature the terms *deputation* and *district* became interchangeable (Taanith 4:67b-68a; 27b). These Israelites also served two weeks, not as priests but as liturgical assistants.

THE HIGH PRIEST

The high priest ruled over the Temple, its institutions, and its hierarchy of ministers but did not regularly officiate at the daily Temple services. He may not even have been religiously versed enough to lead the service! The position was considered so important and sacred, though, that a daily cake offering was sacrificed in his name together with the regular offerings in the Temple (Shekalim 2:14; Tamid 1:3). According to Talmudic tradition, he did involve himself at times in Sabbath and festival worship, and he was always the central figure in the observance of Yom Kippur.

He was appointed by Herod and often won his office through treachery or bribery. Beginning with the Maccabean revolt and up until the time of Herod, the high priest was the leading religious and political figure in Jerusalem.

1. Edersheim, p. 307.

Dynasties were created as the position was passed from father to son after a lifetime of service. But with the ascent of Herod to the throne came the demise of the priestly dynasties, for Herod began appointing the high priest of his choice for the duration he determined.

Upon Herod's death and the removal of Archelaus, the appointing of the high priest passed to the Roman governors of Jerusalem. But in the final generation of the Temple prior to A.D. 70, the Roman governors once again allowed Agrippa II to choose the high priest. According to the Talmud, there were a number of wealthy priestly families from whom the high priest was usually chosen year by year: the Boethus family, the Phiabi family, and the family of Anan (Yoma 18a; Yevamot 61a). The position of the high priest usually went to the family that was the highest bidder. There was also a custom whereby the ex-high priest kept his additional rights to dignity and status much like the pension and dignity attributed to an ex-president of the United States. So there came into being a high priestly clique of wealthy families who were usually Sadducees and were primarily loyal to Rome. This priestly aristocracy of wealthy families tyrannized the people.[2]

The Jewish people's hatred of this high clique was evident during the time of the great revolt in A.D. 70. It is said that when the zealots dominated Jerusalem, they expelled all such families, killed a number of them, and chose a high priest from among the ordinary priests. His name was Phineas ben Samuel, a stone mason by profession, a relative by marriage to the family of Hillel. Phineas ben Samuel was the last Jewish high priest to officiate at the Temple.[3]

Occasionally the high priest would show himself to the worshiping people on the Sabbath or a New Moon. What a sight he must have been, his robes and golden crown shim-

2. Safrai and Stern, vol. 2, pp.600-612.
3. *Encyclopedia Judaica,* vol. 13, p. 1187.

mering in the soft glow of the Temple's white marble, the "self-appointed" representative of God! Even the people's awareness of his corruption might have faded just slightly at a time like that.

THE PREPARATION OF THE PRIEST

But on the great day of Yom Kippur, the high priest was to remove his golden vestments and dress himself in the white linen robes of an ordinary priest. On the week preceding that holy day he was responsible to officiate as a common priest at all daily Temple services. The Jewish leadership felt it necessary to ensure his familiarity with the rituals, that he might not make any errors when conducting the regular Temple service on the Day of Atonement.[4] One further precaution was cleansing the high priest with the ashes of the red heifer twice during the seven-day period, just in case he had somehow come in contact with a corpse that would have defiled him (Numbers 19:13).

An understudy high priest was similarly prepared, lest the high priest become disqualified and Israel be left with no one to atone for them before God.

On the week before Yom Kippur, the high priest left his home and set up residence in his special quarters on the Temple mount. There, the rabbis of the Sanhedrin made sure he was versed in the biblical mandates for the Day of Atonement.

The great Sanhedrin of seventy-one members delivered him to the small Sanhedrin, a judicial court of twenty-three members. This smaller court read him the entire portion of Leviticus 16 and Numbers 29:7-11, making sure he knew exactly how to conduct the Yom Kippur ritual sacrifices. The small Sanhedrin then required him to recite

4. Edersheim, p. 308.

the passages just read. "My lord high priest, recite with thine own mouth in case thou hast forgotten or lest thou hast never learned" (Yoma 1:3). The distrust of the Jewish people towards the Roman-appointed high priest was distinctly evident in these and other precautions taken against his possible ignorance.

On the night before Yom Kippur, the people enjoyed great feasts in preparation for the coming fast day, but the high priest was not allowed such indulgence. He was given a bare minimum of food, lest a heavy meal make him drowsy; for on the night before Yom Kippur, he was not allowed to sleep. The next day's events were too important to allow the central figure to be at all unprepared. So the high priest, with the assistance of several young rabbis, was kept awake throughout the night.

Passages were read to him from the prophetic books in the Scriptures, with the thought that since they were less familiar readings, they might spur his interest and keep him awake. If he was versed enough, he was asked to read as well and even expound the Scripture to his young companions. Should he become so drowsy that he could not keep awake, he was made to stand in his bare feet on the cold marble floor, that the shock might revive him for continued study and prayer. Young priests were assigned to sit by the high priest, and if, by chance, he began falling asleep they were charged to snap their fingers and say to him, "My lord, high priest, stand up and expel [sleep] this once on the floor" (Yoma 1:7), assuming that once the high priest touched the cold marble floor he would be instantly awakened. The high priest had to be thoroughly prepared for his responsibilities on the following day.

Later that evening, the elders of the priesthood took the high priest to the upper chamber of the house of Abtinas, the priestly dynasty charged with the preparation of incense. They left the high priest there after making him

swear: "My lord, high priest, we are delegates of the court
and thou art our delegate of the court. We adjure thee by
Him who made His name to dwell in this house that thou
shalt not change ought of all that which we have said to
thee" (Yoma 1:5).

THE YOM KIPPUR SERVICE

Usually, the Temple services would begin at dawn, but
on the Day of Atonement, pious Jews arrived while the
Temple courts were still in darkness. A hush of anticipa-
tion filled the air as the high priest stepped forward, with
the first rays of dawn, to initiate the Day of Atonement.

THE CLEANSING AND PRIESTLY GARMENTS

In fulfillment of the Scriptures, the high priest was to
bathe himself before officiating, symbolizing his desire to
be pure before God. Usually a priest was only required to
wash his hands and feet, but on this day, the high priest
bathed his entire body five times and cleansed his hands
and feet another ten!

The first bathing was done in full view of the people
(with a curtain of linen drawn between for modesty), that
they might witness his fulfillment of the biblical command.
Having removed his ordinary clothes and washed, he don-
ned the golden garments of the high priest, ready to perform the morning sacrifice.

What a sight he must have been, resplendent in gold
garments with a jeweled shield on his breast and a golden
diadem on his head, bearing the inscription "Holy to the
Lord" (Exodus 28:36)!

THE REGULAR MORNING SERVICE

In splendid pageantry, he officiated at the regular
morning service, the golden bells hanging from the hem of

his purple robe jingling with his every move. In full view of the people, he set in order the golden candelabra, placed incense on the altar, and officiated at the regular morning sacrifice. How relieved they must have been to see the priest alive and competent in his duties! At the end of the service, the high priest removed his ceremonial robes, bathed himself again, and reappeared before the people in the white linen garments representing his purity before God.

A PERSONAL CONFESSION

The sacrificial animals, which the high priest had inspected for cleanness the previous day, were readied at the Temple altar, while the bull of the sin offering was brought to him. This bull was to make atonement for the high priest and his household, an essential step lest the high priest's own sins void the sacrifice made for the nation. Facing the sacrificial bull, he placed his hands upon its head and recited his confession:

> I pray, O eternal! I have done wrong, I have transgressed, I have sinned before Thee, both I and my house; I pray, O eternal! Forgive, I pray, the iniquities, and the transgressions, and the sins, which I have wrongly committed, and which I have transgressed, and which I have sinned before thee, both I and my house, as it is written in the Law of Moses, Thy servant, For on this day shall atonement be made for you to cleanse you; from all your sins you shall be clean before the Lord. (Yoma 3:8)

Three times in this prayer did the high priest utter the ineffable Name of God, which was not to pass from human lips on any other occasion, lest His Holy Name be taken in vain. When the people heard this awesome utterance, they fell with faces to the ground, exclaiming, "Blessed be His name, the glory of His kingdom is forever and ever" (Yoma

3:8). The Tetragrammaton was pronounced ten times during the Yom Kippur ritual, each time eliciting a similar response from the people. This was no insignificant reaction, for a Jewish person was not allowed to prostrate himself except on this the holiest day in the year.

THE TWO GOATS

The bull was led away for the moment as the high priest turned to face the two goats readied for him, goats almost identical in size and appearance. He then took two golden lots from an urn, one marked "for the Lord" and one "for *azazel*," and placed one upon the head of each animal, sealing their fate. It was considered a good omen if the lot marked "for the Lord" was drawn by the priest in his right hand, but for forty years prior to the destruction of the Temple, the lot "for the Lord" appeared on the left (Yoma 39a). This omen struck the Israelites with fear of impending doom.

The goat "for the Lord" waited while the high priest turned to the goat destined "for *azazel*" and tied a crimson sash around its horns. Soon that goat would assume symbolically the sins of the Jewish people and be led into the wilderness to its death. With this ceremony, the second part of the Yom Kippur service ended, and the third, the most awesome portion, was about to begin.

ATONEMENT FOR THE PRIESTHOOD

The high priest once more approached the sacrificial bull. He placed his hands upon its head and recited the same confession he had previously. This time, he added the phrase "and the sons of Aaron, Thy holy tribe," extending the sacrifice to include the entire priesthood of Israel.

As the Scriptures demanded, he made intercession for himself and the priests before he could approach the Lord seeking forgiveness for Israel (Leviticus 16:6). Having confessed his sins and again pronounced the Holy Name of God, the high priest then slaughtered the bull, pouring its blood into a basin. The blood was handed to an assistant priest to stir lest it coagulate, for it was not to be used just yet.

ENTRANCE INTO THE HOLY OF HOLIES

Filled with fear, the high priest prepared to enter the Holy of Holies with the golden ladle of incense and hot coals taken from the altar. On other days, it was proper to use a silver censer, but on Yom Kippur he used gold. The Mishna tells us that the gold was to be red rather than yellow, a much more rare and precious type of gold.

The high priest then entered the holy place and slowly advanced, parting the heavy drape that separated him from the Holy of Holies. Trembling, he entered. According to the Mishna, the curtain that separated the holy place from the Holy of Holies was folded. The priest walked north between the curtains and then turned south walking along the curtain until he was at the Ark, or at least where the Ark used to be. The chamber, lit only by the glow of the burning coals, was empty, for the Mercy Seat, the golden cherubim, and the Ark of the Covenant had disappeared, and along with them the Shekinah presence of the Lord. The items had been taken into captivity in Babylon and were never seen again (2 Kings 24:13; 2 Chronicles 36.7). All that remained in this sacred chamber was one barren rock, three fingers high, known as the Foundation Stone. The Mishna states, "After the ark was taken away a stone remained there from the time of the early prophets, and it was called Shetijah. It was higher than the ground by three finger breadths" (Yoma 5:2). It was as if the heart of the Holy of Holies had been removed.

The priest should have pulled back the curtain of the Holy of Holies and shouted to the waiting Israelites, "Ichabod! The glory of the Lord has departed, and we must repent until the cloud of His presence again fills the Holy of Holies." Instead, the elaborate ritual of atonement was followed, in hope that somehow God would be gracious enough to forgive from afar.

To comply with the ritual, the high priest tossed the incense upon the glowing coals, filling the emptiness of the Holy of Holies with a cloud of smoke. Quickly, he retreated backwards into the holy place and recited a short prayer. The priest was eager to show himself once more to the congregation, who waited outside in hushed silence, dreading the thought that the high priest's service might be unacceptable and he might be struck dead by the Lord. His failure would render the entire nation of Israel unclean and unforgiven.

When the high priest emerged, the gathered multitude breathed a sigh of relief as he continued with the sacrificial ritual. Taking the blood of the bull from the priest who was still stirring it, the high priest then returned to the Holy of Holies and sprinkled the blood on the stone, as he would have done upon the Mercy Seat, one time towards heaven and seven times downward. He counted these sprinklings carefully in a prescribed fashion, lest an error in counting render them unacceptable. It is said that as the priest sprinkled the blood he would count in the following manner: "One," whereupon he sprinkled the blood upwards toward where the Mercy Seat had been; then as he sprinkled the blood seven times downward he would count, "one and one, one and two, one and three," and so forth to prevent any mistake or miscounting.

After this, he left the holy place once more to face the congregation, who observed as he slaughtered the goat designated "for the Lord." Taking its blood in a basin, he entered the Holy of Holies for the third time, sprinkled the blood as before, and stepped out again. He then sprinkled the great curtain with the blood of the bull and of the goat, mixed the two bowls together and sprinkled the golden incense altar in the holy place. When he finished, he poured the remainder of the mixed blood on the corner of the great altar outside. The Temple area itself was not ritually clean.

THE "AZAZEL"

The Yom Kippur blood sacrifice was now completed, but more remained to be done, as the goat marked "for *azazel*" still awaited its fate. The scapegoat was the second part of the sin offering, for indeed the two goats were considered one offering.

The high priest approached the goat and laid his hands upon its head, reciting the same confession as before, only leaving out "I and my household and the sons of Aaron, Thy holy tribe" and confessing instead for "Thy people, the House of Israel."

> We pray, O eternal! We have done wrong, we have transgressed, we have sinned before Thee, Thy people, the House of Israel; We pray, O eternal! Forgive, we pray, the iniquities, and the transgressions, and the sins, which we have wrongly committed, and which we have transgressed, and which we have sinned before thee, Thy people, the House of Israel, as it is written in the Law of Moses, Thy servant, for on this day shall atonement be made for you to cleanse you; from all your sins you shall be clean before the Lord. (Yoma 3:8)

He spoke these words towards the sanctuary, but as he recited the final phrase, "you shall be clean," he turned and faced the people, who fell on their faces and responded once more, "Blessed be His name, the glory of His kingdom is forever and ever."

The high priest now remained in the Temple, while another priest was called to lead away the sin-laden goat to a steep cliff in the wilderness. An elaborate system of es-

corts was prepared to assure that the goat reached its desti-
nation. A course was established dividing the distance
between Jerusalem and the beginning of the wilderness
into ten intervals, each interval being a half Sabbath's journey from the other. The total amount was computed at
ninety *ris,* approximately twelve miles, as a *ris* was approximately two-fifteenths of a mile. At the end of each interval was a small station where the man leading the goat
to the wilderness could stop and rest. One of those tending
the station would then accompany the man leading the
goat away to the next station.

When the goat finally arrived at the precipice, the attending priest removed the red sash from its head and divided it, returning half to the animal's horns and tying the
other half to a protrusion on the cliff. He then pushed the
animal backwards over the cliff, sending it, bearing Israel's
sins, to its death.

In connection with this ceremony, an interesting tradition arose, which is mentioned in the Mishna. A portion
of the crimson sash was attached to the door of the Temple
before the goat was sent into the wilderness. The sash
would turn from red to white as the goat met its end, signaling to the people that God had accepted their sacrifice
and their sins were forgiven. This was based on the verse in
Isaiah where the prophet declared: "Come now, and let us
reason together," says the Lord, "though your sins are as
scarlet, they will be as white as snow; though they are red
like crimson, they will be like wool" (Isaiah 1:18). The
Mishna tells us that forty years before the destruction of
the Temple, the sash stopped turning white. That, of course,
was approximately the year Christ died.

According to the Talmud, the destruction of the Temple did not come as a total surprise to the Jewish people. In
fact, the Talmud records that four ominous events occurred approximately forty years before the destruction of
the Temple. Those four events were to warn the rabbis of

the Temple's impending doom. According to Jewish tradition, all four of these signs came to pass. The four signs were (Yoma 39a, b):

1. The lot for the Lord's goat did not come up in the right hand of the high priest.
2. The scarlet cord tied to the door of the Temple on the Day of Atonement stopped turning white after the scapegoat had been cast over the precipice.
3. The westernmost light on the Temple candelabra would not burn. It is believed that this light was used to light the other lights of the candelabra.
4. The Temple doors would open by themselves. The rabbis saw this as an ominous fulfillment of Zechariah 11:1, "Open thy doors, O Lebanon, that fire may devour thy cedars." The opening of the doors to let in the consuming fire foretold the destruction of the Temple itself by fire.

The sages drew two conclusions from these warnings. First, they realized that the destruction of the Temple was God's judgment upon the Jewish people for ungodliness. Second, they perceived the warnings as God's way of giving them time to prepare for the restructuring of Judaism around the synagogue.

THE CLOSING OF THE SERVICE

When he completed the Temple service, the high priest had a few more duties before the day's events were finished. Once he learned of the death of the *azazel* goat, he entered the synagogue on the Temple grounds and began the reading of the Torah, with much the same ritual as is observed in synagogues today. The high priest had been prepared for this by the elders, lest in his ignorance he should not be able to recite the Scriptures that speak of the Day of Atonement.

According to the Mishna the high priest read publicly those passages of Scripture bearing on the Day of Atonement and pronounced eight benedictions: "For the Law, and for the service, and for the thanksgiving, and for the pardon of sin, and for the Temple [that it would remain forever], and for Israel [its safety and the continuance of a king among them] and for Jerusalem [which, in effect, was a prayer for the restoration of the kingdom] and for the priests [that what they did in their sacred service would be acceptable to God], and for other matters of prayer" (Yoma 7:1).

After the reading, the high priest retired, removed his white robes, and washed himself, again assuming his golden garments in order to officiate at the *Musaf,* or additional sacrifice service. Once this was finished, he removed his golden robes, bathed yet once more, dressed in the white garments, and entered the Holy of Holies one last time to remove the fire-pan and the ladle of incense.

THE EVENING SERVICE

The high priest's duties were not finished yet, for though he completed the special Yom Kippur service, he still had to conduct the regular Temple service, which was performed at sunset. For this, he once again washed and changed into his golden robes, and only after the service was finished did he wash a last time and return to his regular garments. As he went back to his home, the priest was surrounded by a crowd of people who fought for the coveted position of being near him. Later that evening, he threw a great feast for the high-caste priests and aristocrats of society.

There was a tremendous sense of relief and rejoicing among the Israelite crowds as preparations began for the feast of Tabernacles, a festival and celebration of joy. Tradition has it that on this night the young maidens of Jerusalem, all dressed in white lest the rich be esteemed above the poor, went out to the vineyards where the young men waited to look for a suitable wife.

No doubt the celebration of Yom Kippur was a mixed festival, as the people felt sorrow for their sin and joy in the knowledge of sins forgiven. But mostly, Yom Kippur was a day of apprehension, fear, and doubt. At no other time of the Jewish year was the frailty of man so vividly displayed. The Israelites entrusted their national forgiveness to the perfect priestly performance of a grossly imperfect high priest.

Even after the elaborate rituals of the day were precisely followed, the forgiveness won was short-lived, only to be nullified by the act of sin certain to be committed by every Israelite on the eleventh of Tishri. After all, neither Jew nor Gentile could possibly live even one day in holy perfection. The day must be observed every year.

Worship in Herod's Temple was empty and incomplete. The presence of the Lord did not fill the Temple at the time of Christ. After all the intricate rituals were followed, the high priest would enter the Holy of Holies only to be confronted by a cold reminder of the absence of the Shekinah glory.

But God did not remove His presence forever. He did more than could have been expected. He came and dwelt with us in the flesh. Rather than limit His presence to the Holy of Holies, He walked among His people to be seen by all. And the forgiveness He provided would not be "once a year" but a sacrifice that need never be repeated. For Jesus was both the perfect high priest *and* the perfect sacrifice.

10
Jewish Observance of Yom Kippur

PREPARATION FOR THE DAY

Yom Kippur, the Day of Atonement, is the most revered of Israel's holy days. The synagogue is filled past its capacity with worshipers. Even marginally religious Jews will attend services on this day. Scattered among the people can be seen pious worshipers praying, sobbing, and beating their breasts in outward demonstrations of repentance.

The Day of Atonement does not arrive suddenly and without warning. The Jewish people spend Elul, the month before the Day of Atonement, preparing their hearts. The New Moon and Sabbaths of Elul are more solemn than those of the months preceding it.

THE TEN DAYS OF AWE

When the month of Tishri arrives, the feast of Rosh Hashanah begins the sober countdown to Yom Kippur known as the Ten Days of Awe. During these days, the Jewish people are commanded by the rabbis to begin the process of repentance: "The Holy One, blessed be He, said to Israel: Remake yourselves by repentance during the ten days between New Year's Day and the Day of Atonement, and on the Day of Atonement I will hold you guiltless, regarding you as a newly made creature" (Pesikta Rabbati 40:5).

The number *ten* may symbolize perfection, and the restoration of perfect harmony between God and man is the thrust of this most sacred day of the year. The Ten Days of Repentance conclude on the tenth of Tishri (Yom Kippur). A moving confession of sins (the Viddui) is recited ten times on the Day of Atonement to coincide with the tradition that the Temple high priest pronounced the name of God ten times when he invoked divine pardon (Yoma 39b).

Yom Kippur also recalls the Ten Commandments, which, according to Jewish tradition, are personified and serve as advocates before the supreme judge on behalf of the children of Israel.

Judaism teaches that on the first day of Tishri, the New Year, a heavenly judgment takes place; the sentence for the coming year hangs in the balance during the next ten days and is finally sealed on the Day of Atonement.

During these ten days, the religious often fast in contrition until noon, except on the Sabbath and on the eve of Yom Kippur, days on which fasting is prohibited.

SHABBAT SHUVAH: THE SABBATH OF REPENTANCE

The Sabbath that falls in those ten days has a special name, *Shabbat Shuvah*, the "Sabbath of Repentance," and is observed far more stringently than other Sabbaths. It is a Sabbath of turning from sin and preparing for the coming judgment.

PREPARATION RITUALS

The rabbis knew the fast on the Day of Atonement would be difficult to bear, so they declared it a religious duty to eat sumptuously the day before. He who does so for the sake of fulfilling a commandment is regarded as if he fasted also on that day. The noon meal is served early so an even larger meal can be eaten before the fast. This early meal may consist of traditional Jewish dishes such as *kreplach* (three-cornered dough pockets filled with meat), chicken soup, and carrot *tzimmes* (a sweet stew or pudding). The evening meal is a large one, the last food tasted before the approaching all-day fast.

THE RITUAL BATH

It is customary for religious Jews to go to the *mikvah*, or ritual bath, for cleansing on the day before Yom Kippur. The more religious will recite a confession while in the water, preparing themselves for the public confession in the synagogue later that evening.

AN EXTREME TRADITION

One tradition that is no longer practiced but was common in Eastern Europe in centuries gone by is the tradition of *malkut*, or flogging. The elders and pious men would come to the synagogue and prostrate themselves on the floor wearing a heavy overcoat, while a local poor man would symbolically flog them with a leather strap while reciting a scriptural "sentence" for their sins from Psalm 78:38, "But He, being compassionate, forgave their iniquity, and did not destroy them; and often He restrained His anger, and did not arouse all His wrath."

This sentence, which contains thirteen words in the Hebrew, is recited three times, symbolic of the thirty-nine lashes inflicted upon sentenced criminals in ancient times. The ritual was often carried out so quickly that the repentant person barely had time to confess his sins before his turn was finished. He paid a small fee to the flogger and left, having symbolically been punished for his sins.

GIVING TO CHARITY

In the synagogue, long tables were covered with alms plates for every charity in town, for giving to charity is a central theme of the Day of Atonement. Many beggars waited outside the synagogue, certain to receive charity from worshipers eager to perform last-minute good deeds that might tip the heavenly balance in their favor and assure them prosperity in the coming year.

THE KAPPAROT

Another custom that was practiced by the masses but has largely become a thing of the past (except among orthodox communities) is the ritual of *kapparot*. In remembrance of the ancient Temple sacrifice, a pious Jew would take a white fowl (a rooster for males and a hen for females) and wave it over his head three times, while reciting the following formula: "This is a substitute for me; this is in exchange for me; this is my atonement. This cock (or hen) shall be consigned to death, while I shall have a long and pleasant life and peace."[1] The bird was then slaughtered and given to the poor or eaten for the evening meal and its value contributed to the less fortunate.

Some religious modern-day Jews, while not actually performing this ritual, nevertheless participate in a less bloody form: a handkerchief with money tied in it is swung around the head three times while a similar phrase is recited.

The ceremony of kapparot is a substitutionary sacrifice. That is precisely the reason learned rabbis have opposed it through the ages. Faced with the immense popularity of the tradition, yet knowing that the Bible forbade sacrifice outside of the Temple, the rabbis attempted to

1. Julius H. Greenstone, *Jewish Feasts and Fasts* (Philadelphia: Chautauqua Society, 1945), p. 27.

limit and control the similarities between the kapparot ceremony and the Temple sacrifices. Nevertheless, in the minds of many pious Jews, the kapparot filled the vacuum left by the destruction of the Temple. It points to the continuing role of substitutionary atonement in Judaism.

SPECIAL CLOTHING

Before the setting of the sun that signals the beginning of the Day of Atonement, the people gather in the synagogue, many dressed in white *kittels,* or robes, for preparatory prayers. The same kittel will eventually become the worshiper's funeral shroud. A white garment is worn as a symbol of a humble and contrite heart and confidence in God's ability to forgive sins. Even women will sometimes wear white clothes in honor of the day. Perhaps that is the reason the white-garbed Yom Kippur worshiper is likened in Jewish tradition to the ministering angels whose sinless record is as white as snow (Isaiah 1:18). Men wrap themselves in prayer shawls, which are not allowed to be worn at evening services but may be used on this occasion since the service officially begins before sunset.

THE EVENING SERVICE

Some worshipers carry a candle to the synagogue on the eve of Yom Kippur, chanting, "Light is sown like seed for the righteous and gladness for the upright in heart" (Psalm 97:11). The candles memorialize the souls of deceased loved ones, thus atoning for their sins. At home, a similar candle burns. This custom is defended by a Bible passage that likens a man's soul to a glowing candle: "The spirit of man is the lamp of the Lord, searching all the innermost parts" (Proverbs 20:27). The lights from the candles also remind the people of the light of the law, which Moses brought down from Mount Sinai on Yom Kippur.

As people enter the synagogue, they begin swaying and chanting, preparing their hearts for the solemn service to come. Even children sense the feeling of awe that grips the adults on this fearful day. Suddenly, the congregation is hushed with expectation as the ark is opened and a white curtain drawn, revealing the scrolls of the law draped in white. White, the traditional color of the season, symbolizes purity and atonement. In some congregations the scrolls are removed and carried by the elders to be kissed by repentant worshipers, who vow to honor the law in the coming year.

Kol Nidre: The Canceling of Vows

As the scrolls are returned to the ark, the cantor begins chanting the familiar, plaintive melody of the Kol Nidre, described by Tolstoy as "one that echoes the story of the great martyrdom of a grief-stricken nation." It is a melody filled with deep sadness, reaching into the soul to draw out the hidden longings of man.[2] The melody has also found its way into the work of such non-Jewish composers as Beethoven (the penultimate movement of the G Minor Quartet, opus 131, and the first movement of the Trio, opus 9, no. 3) and Bruch (the well-known composition entitled "Kol Nidre").[3]

This moving Kol Nidre prayer is not actually a part of the Yom Kippur service but rather a prelude, recited before the setting of the sun and the beginning of the holy day. The Hebrew and Aramaic texts speak of a canceling of all vows made by the Jewish person during the coming year:

> All vows, renunciations, promises, obligations, oaths, taken rashly, from this Day of Atonement till the next,

2. Hayyim Schauss, *The Jewish Festivals: History and Observance*, trans. Samuel Jaffe (New York: Schocken, 1975), pp. 152ff.
3. Phillip Goodman, *The Yom Kippur Anthology* (Philadelphia: Jewish Pub. Soc. of America, 1971), p. 95.

may we attain it in peace, we regret them in advance. May we be absolved of them, may we be released from them, may they be null and void and of no effect. May they not be binding upon us. Such vows shall not be considered vows; such renunciations, no renunciations; and such oaths, no oaths.

And may atonement be granted to the whole congregation of Israel and to the stranger who lives among them, for all have transgressed unwittingly.

Forgive the sins of this people in accordance with Thy great mercy, as Thou hast continued to forgive them from the days of Egypt until now. As we have been promised: And the Lord said, I have forgiven, in accordance with Thy plea.[4]

Kol Nidre is chanted three times, each time increasing in volume and intensity, until the synagogue is filled with its mournful melody. "The first time he [the reader] must utter it very softly, like one who hesitates to enter the palace of the King to ask a gift of Him whom he fears to approach; the second time he may speak somewhat louder; and the third time more loudly still, as one who is accustomed to dwell at court and to approach his Sovereign as a friend." (This is as prescribed in the thirteenth-century *Mahzor Vitry.*)

It is easy to understand why Kol Nidre, a prayer canceling all vows, has faced centuries of vehement opposition, both from within Judaism and from without. The outright cancellation of sacred vows can easily be abused.

The Scriptures warn us against taking vows lightly: "Do not be hasty in word or impulsive in thought to bring up a matter in the presence of God. . . . It is better that you should not vow than that you should vow and not pay. Do not let your speech cause you to sin. . . . Rather, fear God" (Ecclesiastes 5:2-7).

4. Ben Zion Bokser, ed., *The High Holyday Prayer Book: Rosh Hashanah and Yom Kippur* (New York: Hebrew Pub., 1959), pp. 258-59.

In twelfth-century Spain, R. Judah ben Barzillai declared the recitation of Kol Nidre to be dangerous. He and other rabbis sensed the danger of some Jewish people believing, in error, that they could make obligations lightly, assuming they would be canceled when this prayer was recited.

The Jewish defense of Kol Nidre was always that the declaration applied only to vows made between man and God, and not to those between man and man. Vows to one's fellow man could be canceled only with that person's consent, and vows made in a court of law could not be annulled at all. Chief Rabbi Hertz, in his commentary on the Pentateuch, says:

> Altogether aside from imbecile and rash minds, men in time of danger or under momentary impulse would make vows which they could not fulfill. . . . In such cases, the rabbis would consider it their duty to afford a man the facility, under certain definite conditions and restrictions, of annulling his thoughtless or impossible vows. Such annulment could never be effected by himself, but only by a Bet Din of three learned men in the Law, after they had carefully investigated the nature and bearing of the vow, and had become convinced that its purpose was not, on the one hand, self-improvement, nor did it, on the other, infringe upon the rights of others. For not all vows or oaths could be absolved. A vow or oath that was made to another person, even be that person a child or a heathen, could not be annulled except in the presence of that person and with his consent; while an oath which a man had taken in a court of justice could not be absolved by any other authority in the world.[5]

We do not know the origins of the Kol Nidre chant. Though some have attempted to trace Kol Nidre as far back as the eighth century, it is difficult to do so. Some believe that Kol Nidre was a prayer originated by Jews who were

5. Cited in Goodman, p. 87.

forced to convert to Christianity. Though this cannot be proved, it is possible that some Jewish people used this recitation to absolve themselves from vows made under coercion, such as when the Marranos were forced to renounce their religion and accept the "Christian" faith of Spain. The forced converts would secretly remain faithful to Judaism and continue to observe Yom Kippur. The chant of Kol Nidre expressed their grief over their apostasy and sought God's forgiveness for their unwilling vows.[6]

THE DAY OF ATONEMENT

The rabbis developed a great number of prohibitions for the Day of Atonement, lest a Jewish person unwittingly transgress on this day. One ancient writing summarizes it this way: "The following are prohibited on the Day of Atonement: partaking of food, drinking, washing, anointing, wearing shoes, and sexual intercourse. It is also forbidden to do any manner of work and to carry objects, as on the Sabbath" (Kitzur Shulhan Arukh 133).

There are, of course, exceptions to these rules. For example, the rabbis tell us that one who is ill may wash in his usual manner, and a bride may clean her face so as not to be repulsive to her husband.

THE FAST

Yom Kippur is a day of severe fasting. According to the rabbis, the fast of this day brings one near to the angels, because it is spent in humility and contrition, standing, kneeling, praising, and singing. In fasting, man denies his physical faculties and devotes himself entirely to the spiritual. It is almost as if the animal element in him had disappeared (Kuzari 3:5). But there are some who are excused from fasting on Yom Kippur: a child who is not yet old

6. Goodman, p. 93.

enough to know the commandments need not fast, nor a pregnant woman if she craves food, nor an ill man if he feels he needs the sustenance.

THE LITURGY

The many customs and traditions that set apart the Day of Atonement from all other days are found in the liturgy of the day. The donning of the tallit for the evening service, the white robes worn by the leaders, the removal of the Torah scrolls from the ark—all create an atmosphere of deep solemnity.[7]

THE PRAYER BOOK

The Day of Atonement and Rosh Hashanah share their own unique prayerbook, the *Mahzor*. It reflects centuries of Jewish wisdom and writings, containing psalms and prayers from the days of the Temple, the Middle Ages, and also recent times. In reciting the Yom Kippur service, the Jewish worshiper senses his connection with the eternal truths experienced by his ancestors. Through prayers and resolutions, he seeks to win God's favor for the following year.

The *Union Prayer Book*, used by Reform Jews, contains a touching prayer for Yom Kippur:

> In deep humility and contrition I make supplication unto Thee, my God and my Father, on this holiest of days. Conscious of my frailties and my shortcomings, I seek Thee with the hope in my heart that I shall find forgiveness for my sins, for I know that Thou art merciful and loving, long-suffering and abundant in pardoning. . . .
>
> Accept Thou with favor my prayer for forgiveness, my confession which I make before Thee. May the words

7. Goodman, p. 99.

of my mouth and the meditation of my heart be acceptable before Thee, my Rock and my Redeemer. Amen.[8]

CONFESSION OF SINS

The confession of sins is the high point of the Yom Kippur liturgy. Judaism provides for confession, but it is done in congregational unison, naming not one's own sins but those that make man in general stumble.

This recitation of sins, repeated ten times throughout the day's liturgy, contains in Hebrew an alphabetical list of offenses, two for each letter, with a summary by categories of all religious failures: "God and God of our fathers, pardon our sins on this Day of Atonement. Let our sins and transgressions be removed from Thy sight. . . . O my God, before I was created I was nothing, and now that I have been created, what am I? In life I am dust, and more so when I fall prey to death. When I measure my life in Thy presence, I am confused and I am ashamed. Help me, O God and God of my fathers, to steer clear of sin. And as for my past sins, purge me of them in Thy great mercy, but, I pray, not through severe and painful disease."[9]

As each sin is mentioned, the worshiper beats his heart with his fist. Even though he may not personally have committed that sin, he takes upon himself the guilt that results from his being part of a sinful nation. Every worshiper must recite the complete confession as written in the prayer book. If he did commit a sin specified in the confession, the rabbis say he should experience an inner pang when reciting it. And if a sin he committed is not mentioned in the confession, he does not have to say it

8. *Union Prayer Book for Jewish Worship*, rev. ed., pt. 2 (New York: Central Conference of American Rabbis, 1962), pp. 212-14.
9. Bokser, pp. 269-74.

aloud but rather he should feel guilt and acknowledge it with grief.

PRAYERS FOR FORGIVENESS

"May Our Entreaty Rise to Thee" (*Yaaleh Tahanunenu*) is another Hebrew prayer, written as an acrostic, that makes a soul-stirring plea that the prayers of Israel ascend to heaven at nightfall and arrive before God's throne at dawn, so that salvation and reconciliation may come at dusk.[10] This cycle reflects the rhythm of the twenty-four-hour Yom Kippur service.

Another prayer, "Forgiven" (*Salahti*), also an acrostic, is recited during the evening service. In this prayer, the worshiper admits that his evil inclination has taken him captive and pleads with God to show His grace and mercifully respond with the reply "Forgiven!" This becomes the refrain of each of the poem's verses.

The sinner then pleads with God to ignore the claims of Satan, who accuses him at the heavenly courts held during this season, and rather listen to a good angel who intercedes for Israel and advocates their acquittal.[11] An additional prayer, "We Are Thy People" (*Anu Ammekha*), begins with expressions of intimacy between God and Israel, taken from various parts of the Bible. Then it takes a sudden change of tone from confidence to contrition, as the worshiper considers man's stubbornness and God's patience. At the end, the prayer pleads with God for forgiveness, based on the merit of confessed sins.[12]

10. Morris Silverman, ed. *High Holiday Prayer Book* (Hartford: Prayer Book Press, 1951), p. 227.
11. Bernard Martin, *Prayer in Judaism* (New York: Basic Books, 1968), p. 221.
12. Max Arzt, *Justice and Mercy: Commentary on the Liturgy of the New Year and the Day of Atonement* (New York: Holt, Rinehart and Winston, 1963), pp. 214-15.

THE PRAYERS FOR THE DEAD

Another prayer that is central to the Day of Atonement liturgy is "May God Remember" (*Yizkor*), more commonly known as the prayer for the dead.

By reciting this prayer, the Jewish person is reminded that man's soul does not die with his body but continues to exist. The way man lives his life on earth has eternal consequences. Yet in Jewish tradition, the prayers, charity, and good deeds of the living are believed to atone for the souls of the dead: "Atone for Your people Israel—this refers to the living; whom You redeemed—this refers to the dead. This teaches that the departed require expiation; therefore charity should be pledged in their name" (Sifri).

It is because of this belief that Jewish people say prayers for the dead and give to charity on their behalf. The memory of a Jewish person continues to live in the lives of those he has influenced. Thus, it is particularly important for children to say these memorial prayers for their parents, resolving to follow in their teachings.[13]

THE TEMPLE SERVICE RELIVED

A high point of the Yom Kippur service occurs as the order of the Temple Service is relived. When the cantor mentions that the people prostrated themselves in the court of the Temple, pious Jews throw themselves to the ground just as their ancestors did in the Temple in Jerusalem when the ineffable name of God was pronounced by the high priest.

The act of kneeling is a prominent feature of the New Year and Day of Atonement services. Jews are forbidden to kneel in worship. On New Year and the Day of Atonement,

13. Louis Jacobs, *A Guide to Yom Kippur* (London: Jewish Chronicle Publications, 1957), pp. 44-46.

however, an exception is made; and a high point of the service is the moment when the entire congregation kneels and falls upon their faces as the cantor intones the ancient words said in tradition to have been composed by Joshua himself upon his entry into the Promised Land: "We bend the knee and prostrate ourselves and make acknowledgment before the supreme King of Kings, the Holy One, blessed be He, who stretched out the heavens and laid the foundations of the earth, whose glorious throne is in the heavens and the home of whose majesty is in the loftiest heights."[14]

YHWH, the Tetragrammaton, is no longer uttered by Jewish people, since the correct pronunciation has been lost to man. Rather than take the name of God in vain by mispronouncing it, the Tetragrammaton is not uttered at all.

THE CLOSING OF THE SERVICE

The last moments of Yom Kippur are extraordinary. As shadows begin to fall over the congregation, the "Closing," or *Neilah*, is recited. Originally this was the name of the concluding ceremony at the Temple, when the great gates were shut and the people dismissed, but through time it has come to mean the closing of the gates of heaven, where a man's judgment is sealed for the following year. As the heavenly gates close, man pleads with God to open them wide again that the people, cleansed of their sins, might once more enjoy God's favor.

As the *Neilah* comes to an end, the people join with the cantor in a final declaration of their faith:

> Hear, O Israel, the Lord is our God, the Lord is One [recited once].

14. Goodman, p. 121.

Blessed be the name of His glorious kingdom forever
and ever [recited three times].
The Lord, He is God [recited seven times].

The first phrase, "Hear O Israel," is pronounced only
once, that the people may not be confused and think there
is more than one God. Then the kingship of God is mentioned three times, referring to His sovereignty over past,
present, and future. And seven times it is affirmed that
"the Lord, He is God" (1 Kings 18:39), as the number seven
emphasizes the perfection of God's nature.

When the sun begins to set, the congregation rises.
This is a solemn moment, as the people realize that their
fates for the year ahead are about to be sealed. The shofar
is blown—one long, resounding blast. And the call of the
trumpet is answered by the congregation's hope, *L'shanah
ha ba'ah birushalayim*, "Next year in Jerusalem!"

Though the people are tired from the day of fasting
and prayers, they do not rush home to eat. First, they ham-
mer the first nail of the Sukkah, the booth for the feast of
Tabernacles that will begin in five days. Only then do they
sit down to a festive meal and break their fast.

On the morning after Yom Kippur, religious Jews make
it a point to wake early and say their prayers, lest Satan
accuse them that once Yom Kippur is over, they become
too lazy to get up for the morning services.

A MESSIANIC TRADITION

There is yet one more point of interest to be found in
the Yom Kippur service. It is an ancient prayer, no longer
found in the Day of Atonement liturgy nor usually read in
the modern observance of the feast. But it has special
meaning to those who believe Jesus is the Suffering Servant spoken of by Isaiah (see Isaiah 53):

Our righteous anointed is departed from us: horror hath seized us, and we have none to justify us. He hath borne the yoke of our iniquities and our transgression, and is wounded because of our transgression. He beareth our sins on his shoulder, that he may find pardon for our iniquities. We shall be healed by His wound, at the time that the Eternal will create Him [the Messiah] as a new creature.[15]

15. *Form of Prayers for Day of Atonement*, rev. ed. (New York: Rosenbaum and Werbelowsky, 1890), pp. 287-88.

11
Atonement Without a Temple

Judaism is a religion of atonement. The Day of Atonement, the most sacred day of the year, speaks to the Jewish person of his dire need to be in right standing with the God of Abraham, Isaac, and Jacob.

The God-ordained method of obtaining atonement, though, was shattered with the destruction of the second Temple in A.D. 70, and the Jewish leadership was faced with a crisis they had not encountered since the Babylonian captivity. There was no longer an altar where the required blood sacrifices could be offered. Without a proper sacrifice, there could be no forgiveness of sins. How could the Day of Atonement, the most crucial day in the Jewish consciousness, continue to be observed? Judaism as a religion stood in peril of being obliterated along with the sacred Temple and sacrificial system.

THE BABYLONIAN CAPTIVITY

This was not the first time that Judaism was without a Temple. The people of Israel dwelt in Babylon for almost seventy years mourning the destruction of the altar of God. How did they survive spiritually? How was atonement made in exile?

Prayer was one method the exiles used to seek the favor of God. Daniel prayed three times a day, the usual hours of prayer at the Temple in Jerusalem (Daniel 6:10,

13). He and the faithful in Babylon cast themselves on
God's mercy, as did Moses after the sin of the golden calf
(Daniel 9:18). Yet they still hoped for the restoration of the
Temple (Daniel 9:17) and the sacrifices required for for-
giveness of sins.

JEWS AND THE TEMPLE SINCE THE EXILE

The rabbis trace the origins of the synagogue to Babylon, where a seminal synagogue system developed. A "non-
sacrificial" approach to God was designed, but it was
acknowledged to be temporary and inadequate. This is evident as virtually the first act of the remnant when they returned to Jerusalem was to construct an altar for sacrifice
(Ezra 3:2-3). And yet the synagogue became an integral
part of the pharisaic heritage, growing to maturity after the
destruction of the second Temple hundreds of years later.

Those Jews who remained in the Diaspora had little
contact with the second Temple other than through the
synagogue liturgy. Some occasionally made pilgrimages to
Jerusalem for the three required feasts but could not do so
every year. Others sent offerings with those who were able
to go up in person.

Meanwhile, the religion of the synagogue garnered increasing strength in the Diaspora communities. The synagogue participants prayed and read the Scriptures just as
was done in the Temple at the times of the sacrifices. Soon,
these prayers came to be regarded as sufficient identification with the sacrifices to avail for those outside of Israel.
Priests and Levites from these communities would go up to
Jerusalem for "reserve" duty once a year, strengthening
the identification of the synagogue with the Temple.

As corruption grew in the Jerusalem hierarchy and a
grass-roots piety developed among the people, the synagogues became an inviting alternative to the Temple, though

the rabbis and Pharisees never severed ties with the Temple nor ceased tithing or offering sacrifices. But the synagogues eventually became the true centers of faith and piety for the people.

Before A.D. 70, the sect of the Pharisees had already begun the process of transferring the sanctity of the Temple and priesthood to themselves. Taking Exodus 19:6 seriously ("You shall be to me a kingdom of priests"), they regarded themselves as priests, their homes as temples, their tables as altars. They did not reject the sacrificial system, but when the Temple was destroyed, they had ready-made methods for atonement to take its place.[1]

The rabbis said, "As long as the Temple stood, the altar atoned for Israel. But now, a man's table atones for him" (Berakhot 55a).

This gives an interesting insight into the New Testament comparison of the Lord's Table with the altar (see Hebrews 13:10; 1 Corinthians 10:16-21). By the time of the destruction of the Temple, most Jews outside of Jerusalem were already worshiping God without the Temple and its altar.

ATONEMENT WITHOUT A TEMPLE

The loss of the Temple was and still is mourned by the Jewish people. Yet life continued. The rabbis established a temporary headquarters in the town of Yavneh. This city, located a few miles south of modern Tel-Aviv, became the site of Judaism's reorganization after the fall of Jerusalem in A.D. 70. The Sanhedrin reconvened in Yavneh, first under the leadership of Rabbi Yohanan ben Zakkai, who was succeeded by Rabban Gamaliel II. The city became a substitute for Jerusalem and was actually visited three times

1. Jacob Neusner, "Judaism in a Time of Crisis," *Judaism,* vol. 21 (Summer 1972), pp. 319-20.

each year by pilgrims from the Dispersion. The sages of Yavneh were instrumental in the writing of the Mishna.[2]

The rabbis who gathered in Yavneh felt they were entrusted with the preservation of Israel. Confronted with the loss of the sacrificial altar, they turned to the Bible in search of other means of atonement. And with the Scriptures as their basis, using accepted rabbinic methods of interpretation, they deduced many alternate forms of atonement. The leaders at Yavneh knew that if Judaism was to continue, it was their task to make Jewish religious life revolve around the synagogue, just as it once had around the Temple itself. Through their human efforts, they hoped to lead the Jewish people once again to peace and reconciliation with God.

BIBLICAL PRECEDENTS FOR FORGIVENESS WITHOUT BLOOD

There are some biblical precedents to be found for atonement and forgiveness without a blood sacrifice.

In Leviticus 5:11-13 a meal offering was substituted for the blood sacrifice to atone for the sins of the poor. This can be attributed to God's grace in not wanting to place forgiveness out of the reach of the poor. But even though there was no blood involved, the sacrifice was still required and had to be offered on the altar. It is not license for bloodless atonement outside of the Temple service.

At Mount Sinai, we see Moses appearing before God to try to atone for the sin of the golden calf (Exodus 32:30). True, here is an example of atonement through repentance and prayer that occurred before the existence of the Tabernacle. But those involved in the sin were still punished by death. Moses' prayer availed to save the nation but not the ones who had sinned. Yet we must keep in mind that Moses threw himself and Israel upon God's mercy—there was no

2. *Encyclopedia Judaica*, vol. 9, pp. 1176-77.

provision in the Torah for this. God was under no obligation to forgive.

There is an instance in Exodus 30:15-16 where a tax is said to atone for the people. The one-half shekel tax provided the funds for the Temple to operate, including, probably, the purchase of the public atonement offerings. The tax was not payment for specific sins and, again, was not a substitute for the Temple service itself but was part of the service that included a blood sacrifice.

There are many references in the prophets that seem to abrogate the need for a blood sacrifice. Some have argued that the priests instituted the sacrificial system, whereas the prophets of Israel fought against it. The following verses are among those used to support this view:

"Obedience is better than sacrifice" (1 Samuel 15:22-23). In this passage, Saul had offered a sacrifice he was told *not* to offer. Samuel was not choosing obedience over sacrifice but was saying that obedience validates sacrifice. Both are necessary.

"I delight in loyalty rather than sacrifice" (Hosea 6:6). Here, God was speaking to an Israel who held an automatic view of sacrifice, whose sacrifices were an abomination because of their wanton disobedience to God. The intent is "I delight in loyalty rather than *merely* sacrifice."

"I did not speak to your fathers . . . concerning burnt offerings. . . . But this is what I commanded them, saying, 'Obey My voice' " (Jeremiah 7:22-23). This does not mean that the sacrificial system was not given by God through Moses. Once again, the people commonly believed that the mere presence and operation of the Temple guaranteed the security of Israel. God says through Jeremiah, "I wasn't talking about sacrifices. I want your obedience first." Jeremiah also says in the Lord's name, "If you listen attentively to Me . . . then [people] will come in bringing sacrifices of thanksgiving to the house of the Lord" (Jeremiah 17:24-

26). Sacrifices are acceptable when the people are in a right relationship with God.

"For Thou dost not delight in sacrifice, otherwise I would give it. . . . The sacrifices of God are a broken spirit" (Psalm 51:16-17). As in the case above, the ritual of sacrifice is not to be regarded as payment for sin. God wants contrition. "*Then* Thou wilt delight in righteous sacrifices" (v. 19, emphasis added). These verses don't argue for atonement without sacrifice but rather say that it must be accompanied by repentance, contrition, and obedience. All elements are necessary.

RABBINIC SUBSTITUTIONS FOR THE SACRIFICIAL SYSTEM

REPENTANCE

The sages tell us that repentance is the path that now leads to atonement. According to Moses Maimonides, repentance atones for all transgressions. He wrote:

> At this time, when the Temple no longer exists, and we have no atonement altar, nothing is left but repentance. Repentance atones for all transgressions. Even if a man was wicked throughout his life and repented at the end, we must not mention anything about his wickedness to him, as it is written, "And as for the wickedness of the wicked, he will not stumble because of it in the day when he turns from his wickedness" (Ezekiel 33:12). Yom Kippur itself atones for those who repent, as it is written, "For it is on this day that atonement shall be made for you. " (Leviticus 16:30; Moses Maimonides, *Mishneh Torah,* Laws of Repentance, 1:3, 2:1, 9-10)

But this repentance must meet certain standards: true repentance must show a genuine regret for the sinful action of the past, a sincere resolve not to sin again, and confession by word of mouth.[3]

This is not a new belief, for during the Temple days repentance was necessary for a sacrifice to be effective: "Neither sin-offering nor trespass offering nor death, nor the Day of Atonement can bring expiation without repentance" (Tosefta Yoma 5:9).

In Jewish teachings, there is a sense of repentance being the ultimate means of atonement. As the rabbis said, "There is nothing greater than repentance" (Deuteronomy Rabbah 2:24). Another quote is: "Great is repentance, for it reaches to the Throne of Glory. Great is repentance, for it makes the Redemption (by the Messiah) to come near. Great is repentance, for it lengthens the years of a man's life" (Yoma 86a). But a person must never sin deliberately with the intention of repenting later, for repentance then will be of no avail. "If one says 'I will sin and repent, I will sin and repent,' he will not be given [from on high] an opportunity to repent. [If he says] 'I will sin and the Day of Atonement will effect atonement,' the Day of Atonement does not effect atonement" (Yoma 8:9).

The sages insist that repentance must be sincere. "Whoever commits a transgression and is filled with shame thereby, all his sins are forgiven him" (Berakhot 12b). And sincere repentance is evidenced by a change of conduct. "If a man, if guilty of a transgression, makes a confession of it but does not amend his behavior, to what is he like? To a man who holds a defiling reptile in his hand. Even if he immerses his body in all the waters of the world,

3. Philo, quoted in Samuel Belkin, *In His Image: The Jewish Philosophy of Man as Expressed in Rabbinic Tradition* (New York: Abelard-Schuman, 1960), pp. 54-55.

his immersion is of no avail to him. However, cast the reptile aside, it immediately avails him; as it is said, 'He who confesses (his sins) and forsakes them will find compassion' " (Proverbs 28:13b; Taanith 16a).

With proper repentance, the rabbis tell us, forgiveness is assured: "He who feels bitter shame and compunction over his sins is sure of obtaining pardon" (Berakhot 12b, Haggigah 5a).[4]

THE DAY OF ATONEMENT

In time, the synagogue ritual of Yom Kippur began to be seen as a replacement for the animal sacrifices of the Temple. The rabbis attributed to the day itself the power to effect atonement, basing their views on Leviticus 16:30: "For it is on this day that atonement shall be made for you to cleanse you; you shall be clean from all your sins before the Lord."

However, as with repentance, they insisted that if one sins intentionally, expecting the Day of Atonement to make atonement, then it will not (Yoma 8:9). The Day of Atonement is thought to make atonement only for sins between man and God. Sins between man and man require the appeasing of one's fellow first (Moses Maimonides, *Mishneh Torah,* Laws of Repentance, 1:3, 2:1, 9-10).

The Talmud clearly teaches that personal suffering may procure atonement: "There are chastenings which purge all the iniquities of man" (Berakhot 5a).

"Let a man rejoice in sufferings more than in happiness; for if a man has lived all his life in happiness, any sin which he may have committed has not been pardoned; but what is pardoned through suffering is forgiven him. Beloved are sufferings, because just as the sacrifices secured acceptance, so do sufferings secure acceptance. Nay, suf-

4. *Jewish Encyclopedia,* p. 278.

ferings bring even greater acceptance, since sacrifices en-
tail money only, while sufferings affect the body" (Sifre
Deuteronomy 32:37b).

According to rabbinic teaching, God punishes the
righteous for their few sins here so that they will receive
only reward in the life to come.[5]

DEATH

The rabbis understood that death was one of the pen-
alties of sin. Yet they went so far as to say that a man's own
death could warrant forgiveness, on the condition that he
truly repented before he died.

The principle of atonement by death is perhaps best
illustrated in the following passage from the Talmud:

> When he [a condemned man] was about ten cubits from
> the place of stoning, they used to say to him, "make thy
> confession," for such is the way of them that have been
> condemned to death to make confession. . . . If he
> knows not how to make his confession, they say to him,
> "Say 'May my death be an atonement for all my sins.' "
> (Sanhedrin 6:2)

The Bible does not accept one's own death as an appropriate form of atonement. The intent of the sacrificial
system was to provide a substitute so the sinner could live,
forgiven and in a harmonious relationship to God. After the
destruction of the Temple, however, death, as the severest
form of suffering, was seen as appropriate atonement for
sins of a serious nature. Death alone, for example, could
atone for the sin of profaning the divine name (Yoma 86a).

5. Ephraim E. Urbach, *The Sages—Their Concepts and Beliefs,* vols. 1
and 2 (Jerusalem: Magnes Press, 1975), p. 204.

CAN DEATH ATONE FOR OTHERS?

This raises the question of rabbinic objection to Christ's death atoning for our sins. In the rabbis' own theology, the death of the righteous had atoning power for others. "As the Day of Atonement atones, so the death of the righteous atones" (Leviticus Rabbah, Ahare Mot, 20:12). Also the following quote: "The death of the righteous weighs as heavily as the burning of the Temple" (Rosh Hashanah 18b).

In fact, they believed that the death of the righteous or innocent could atone for a whole generation. "In an age when there are righteous men in a given generation, the righteous are taken for the generation; in a generation where there are no righteous men, school children are taken" (Shabbat 33b).

A righteous man can also atone for the sins of the unrighteous. But in order to make sure that no one was escaping responsibility for his own transgressions, the warning was issued: "A man must not trust in the work of his ancestors. If a man does not do good in this world, he cannot put his trust in the work of his fathers. No man will eat in the time to come of his fathers' works, but only of his own" (Midrash Psalm 146:3).

How much more could Christ, who lived a perfectly righteous life, make atonement through His death for the sins of the entire world?

DIVINE MERCY

The rabbis say that "wherever there are sins and righteous deeds set against each other in the scale of justice, God inclines [the scale] toward mercy" (Pesikta 26:167a).

Rabbi Hillel taught that those who have no merit of their own are pardoned by divine mercy: "Not in reliance

6. *Jewish Encyclopedia*, p. 278.

upon our merits . . . but trusting in Thy great mercy"
(Yoma 87b).

GOOD DEEDS

Charitable deeds help bring about forgiveness, though
they are not one of the major forms of atonement. The rabbis taught that repentance and works of benevolence together plead for man before God's throne (Shabbat 32a)
and are a shield against punishment (Avot 4:11).

It is said that after the destruction of the Temple, Yohanan ben Zakkai was walking with Rabbi Joshua when the
latter saw the Temple in ruins. He cried out:

> "Woe to us that this is in ruins—the place where the sins
> of Israel were expiated!" Rabban Yohanan ben Zakkai re-
> plied: "My son, be not grieved, we have a means of atone-
> ment that is commensurate with it. Which is this? It is
> the performance of acts of lovingkindness, as it is said,
> 'For I delight in loyalty rather than sacrifice' [Hosea
> 6:6]." (Avot de Rabbi Nathan 4:18)

Yet Yohanan ben Zakkai, the great teacher of Judaism,
himself did not have the personal assurance of salvation.
This pathetic story is told of his dying moments:

> In his last hours, Rabban Yohanan ben Zakkai kept
> weeping out loud. "O master," his disciples exclaimed,
> "O tall pillar, light of the world, mighty hammer, why art
> thou weeping?" "I go to appear before the King of Kings,
> the Holy One, blessed be he . . . moreover I have before
> me two roads, one to paradise and one to Gehenna and I
> *know not* whether He will sentence me to Gehenna or
> admit me into paradise."[7] (Avot de Rabbi Nathan 40a;
> chapter 35, Schechter)

7. Cited in Louis Goldberg, "Whatever Happened to the Substitute
Atonement of the Torah?" in *Issues: A Messianic Jewish Perspective,* 5:7, p. 8.

PRAYER, FASTING, AND CHARITY

The rabbis believed that prayer takes the place of sacrifice (Pesikta 25:165b, Hosea 14:2).

They refer to the fact that Daniel didn't have sacrifices in Babylon (Daniel 4:27) and say that prayer is the true service of worship. In King Ahab and in the people of Nineveh they cite two instances of repentance and prayer combined with fasting as a token of contrition (1 Kings 21:27; Jonah 3:7).[8]

There is an interesting rabbinic comment that equates fasting with the offering of sacrifices upon the altar:

> Rav Sheshet said: "Sovereign of the universe, it is known to Thee that when the Temple was in existence, if a man sinned he would bring a sacrifice of which only the fat and blood were offered up, and he would be granted atonement. Now I have observed a fast and my own fat and blood have been diminished. May it be thy will that my diminished fat and blood be accounted as though I had offered them up before thee on the altar, and do thou show me favor." (Berakhot 17a)

Fasting is seen as an act of self-affliction, affirming a man's sincerity. The man who fasts for his sins is saying by his action, "I do not want to be let off lightly; I deserve to be punished." Yet fasting also must be accompanied by repentance: "Men who fast without repentance shall be ashamed" (Midrash on Psalm 25:5).

By fasting on the Day of Atonement, the needs of the body are left unattended for twenty-four hours, and the Jewish person gives all his concentration to the things of the spirit. This is the meaning of the references in Jewish tradition that Jews are compared to the angels on the Day of Atonement when, clothed in white, they spend the whole day in prayer, contemplation, and worship.

8. *Jewish Encyclopedia,* p. 279.

OTHER FORMS OF ATONEMENT

Alternate means of atonement. The rabbis saw a hierarchy in the seriousness of sins committed, so they developed an elaborate system of alternate means of atonement to compensate for the loss of the sacrificial system. These means are grouped according to the category of sin:

1. Breaking a positive commandment ("thou shalt"). In the case of breaking a positive commandment, repentance was sufficient to effect atonement (Yoma 85b).
2. Breaking a negative commandment ("thou shalt not"). In the case of breaking a negative commandment, repentance served to suspend punishment until the Day of Atonement, which would in itself atone for the sin (based on Leviticus 16:30).
3. Committing a graver sin punishable by death or extirpation. For this, there was need for repentance, which would suspend punishment until the Day of Atonement, and further suffering was needed on the part of the sinner to atone for the transgression (based on Psalm 89:33).
4. Profaning the divine name. This heinous sin required all three methods: repentance, the Day of Atonement, and personal suffering—but all these only served to suspend the punishment. Only the sinner's death could atone for this gravest of all transgressions (based on Isaiah 22:4, "Surely this iniquity shall not be expiated by you till you die"; Yoma 86a).
5. Sinning against another person. Even the Day of Atonement was not sufficient for sins against a fellow man, for the Day of Atonement atones only for sins against God (based on Leviticus 16:30, "all your sins before the Lord"). For sins against a fellow man, restitution and forgiveness are needed (Yoma 8:9). The great Spanish rabbi and "codifier" of Jewish religion, Moses Maimonides, wrote: "Repentance and Yom Kippur effect atone-

ment only for sins committed against God, as when one
has eaten forbidden food; . . . for sins committed against
a fellow man, as when a person either injured or cursed
or robbed his neighbor, he is never pardoned unless he
compensates his neighbor and makes an apology" (Moses
Maimonides, *Mishneh Torah,* Laws of Repentance 1:3,
2:1, 9-10).

Several other forms of atonement are only briefly
mentioned in rabbinic writings but should nevertheless be
pointed out:

1. *The study of the Torah* is thought to be more effective
   than sacrifice, especially when combined with charitable acts (Rosh Hashanah 18a; Yevamot 105a; Leviticus
   Rabbah 25).
2. *The family table* from which the poor received their
   share is thought to bring atonement. The wife is the
   priestess who makes atonement for the house (Berakhot
   55a; Tanhumah, Vayishlah 6).
3. *The meritorious lives of the patriarchs* possess atoning
   power for their descendants (Exodus Rabbah 49).
4. *The Holy Land* has atoning qualities for those who live
   in it or are buried in its soil. This is based on the verse
   "He will atone for His land and His people" (Deuteronomy 32:43; Sifre, Deuteronomy 333; Genesis Rabbah 96;
   Ketubboth 111a; Jerusalem Kilayim 9:32c).
5. *The descent of the wicked into Gehenna* is an atoning
   sacrifice for Israel (Isaiah 43, KJV; cf. Proverbs 21:18).
   This is based on the verse "I gave Egypt for thy ransom,
   Ethiopia and Seba for thee" (Sifre, Deuteronomy 333;
   Exodus Rabbah 11).

All these elaborate methods of atonement are only
hollow substitutes for the altar. Jewish people still ache for

the day when the Temple will be rebuilt and sacrifices restored. That is one reason the Mishna devotes an entire tractate to "Holy Things" (*Kodashim*), a rabbinic guide to the Temple sacrifices.

The traditional messianic hope of the Jewish people includes Israel's victory over the nations, the resurrection of the dead, and the rebuilding of the Temple. This longing for the altar's return is evidence of Judaism's continued belief in the need of blood for atonement.

A Solution

There is a solution to the question, How does one find atonement without the Temple? The solution is found in Jesus. He claimed to be the living Temple (John 2:21). In Him are all the elements of the sacrificial system found. He is the High Priest, the offering, and the altar itself. He shed His blood as a perfect sacrifice forty years before the second Temple was destroyed. The redemption purchased by His death is able to usher both Jews and Gentiles into the presence of the Holy One. The blood shed by Jesus is available to all, today and forever.

12

Forgiven Finally and Forever: The Christian and Yom Kippur

The apostle Paul wrote to the believers in Rome: "But God demonstrates His own love towards us, in that while we were yet sinners, Christ died for us. Much more then, having now been justified by His blood, we shall be saved from the wrath of God through Him" (Romans 5:8-9). A Christian does not have to wonder whether his repentance has been thorough and his good works adequate, because salvation, finally and forever, rests not on his own merits but upon the finished work of Christ. Salvation is God's gift to the believing heart. The apostle wrote that we are "justified as a gift by His grace through the redemption which is in Christ Jesus; whom God displayed publicly as a propitiation in His blood through faith" (Romans 3:25-26).

Christ died for the ungodly, but it was more than an act of ultimate altruism; it was an act of propitiation. The Greek word used here for propitiation (*hilasterion*) is the word that the Septuagint uses to translate the Hebrew word *kapporeth*, or Mercy Seat, the place upon which the high priest sprinkled the blood of the bull and the goat to secure forgiveness for the people of Israel. Whether Paul is equating Jesus Himself with the Mercy Seat or simply linking Christ's sacrifice to the place where atonement was made we are unsure. We do know that Jesus, in His death, did more for our sinful condition than all the high priests and all the bulls and goats ever sacrificed upon the altar.

The atonement purchased by Jesus Christ through the shedding of His blood is received by the believer through faith. That results in justification—right standing with God (Romans 5:1) and gracious access into the presence of the heavenly Father.

For the Christian, Yom Kippur should be a day of great celebration, a day when we remember that Christ died for us (1 Corinthians 15:1-3). It should remind us that salvation is by grace, received by faith, and that even faith is a "gift of God" (Ephesians 2:8-9). We need not worry that our bad deeds may outweigh the good in God's balance scales of judgment. Our salvation rests securely upon God Himself. What freedom and joy we experience, and how gracious He is to save us from sin!

THE BOOK OF HEBREWS AND YOM KIPPUR

The book of Hebrews, more than any other book in the New Testament, portrays Jesus as the fulfillment of Yom Kippur. The book is filled with allusions to the day and detailed descriptions of how the Old Covenant sacrificial system is fulfilled in Christ.

The writer of the book argues convincingly that Jesus is better in every respect than the Old Testament revelation. He does not say that the Old Testament revelation was faulty or inferior. Paul, writing to the Romans (Romans 7:12), expounds on the worthiness of the ancient revelation. Yet he also declared this revelation to be incomplete without Christ (Romans 10:4).

The Old Covenant pointed to the Messiah who would be the perfecter of the faith. Jesus is a better prophet (Hebrews 1:2); He is better than the angels (Hebrews 1:4) and higher in position than Moses himself (Hebrews 3:3-6).

Atonement is superior through Christ because Jesus Himself is uniquely superior. He is a superior high priest; He offers a superior sacrifice and grants us superior access to the presence of God. Understanding these truths will give the Christian a deeper appreciation for Jesus Christ, who is our atonement.

A SUPERIOR HIGH PRIEST

The high priesthood of Jesus can best be appreciated when seen as the fulfillment of the Old Testament high priestly role and then compared to the high priest of the second Temple period. It was no accident that Jesus appeared in Jerusalem when He did. The corruption of the high priesthood at that time was well known. The writer of Hebrews presented God's alternative to the corrupt system, exalting Jesus as the superior messianic High Priest —superior in character and ministry.

A SUPERIOR CHARACTER

The author of Hebrews wrote, "For it was fitting that we should have such a high priest, holy, innocent, undefiled, separated from sinners and exalted above the heavens" (Hebrews 7:26).

The holiness of Christ, as demonstrated in His life, ministry, and resurrection, is evidence of His divine character. The Old Testament high priest, weak because of his flesh, was commanded to wear white garments to symbolize his desire for purity and holiness. But Jesus did not need external symbols; He was perfect forever because He was the Son of God (Hebrews 7:28).

The God of justice, who demanded the shedding of blood for the forgiveness of sin, Himself became a man and shed His own blood to obtain that forgiveness. Isaiah wrote that there would be no other Savior than God Himself: "I, even I, am the Lord; and there is no savior besides Me" (Isaiah 43:11). Jesus is superior in character to the high priest because He shares in the divine nature and *is* God Himself.

The Levitical high priest needed to atone for his own sins before presenting a sacrifice for his people. The writer of Hebrews said, "The high priest enters once a year and not without taking blood which he offers for himself . . . and because of it he was obligated to offer sacrifices for sins, as for the people, so also for himself" (Hebrews 9:7; 5:3). But this was completely unnecessary for Jesus, as He was innocent, without evil according to the standard of God's law (Hebrews 4:15).

Jesus is superior to the second Temple high priests. The customs for preparing the high priest on the Day of Atonement showed the spiritually bankrupt and ungodly character of the office.

The Mishna instructed the elders to have a scholar read and expound the Scriptures to the high priest, who was often incapable of doing so himself. Jesus, the Word of God incarnate (John 1:14), was the author of the sacred texts and certainly needed no man to teach Him the Scriptures.

The rite of purification for the high priest is outlined in Leviticus 16. He was instructed to wear white garments symbolizing his holy office and to wash himself with ceremonial washings and so purify his heart before God.

By the time of Christ, these requirements had been greatly expanded. The first-century high priest was to wash himself five times during the Day of Atonement ritual. He was sprinkled with the ashes of the red heifer twice during his seven days of internment, just in case he had come in contact with a corpse before his time of preparation. The ritual purification of the high priest was complex because the Jews were terrified that he would be found unacceptable to God, making his offerings of atonement invalid.

But Christ was in no need of ritual purification. It was unnecessary for Him to endure the ritual washings of the high priest or the sprinkling of ashes from a red heifer. Nothing external could enhance the purity of His character. Again, the author of Hebrews demonstrated Christ's worthiness to be our great messianic High Priest when he wrote, "Therefore, He had to be made like his brethren in all things, that He might become a merciful and faithful high priest in things pertaining to God, to make propitiation for the sins of the people" (Hebrews 2:17).

Unlike His first-century counterpart, Jesus lived among the common people and understood their troubles. He did not remove Himself as part of a religious aristocracy. By nature He was merciful, although He discovered through bitter experience that the high priests knew no mercy. He was also faithful and committed to the difficult task God had called Him to do—to be offered up as an atonement for the sins of His people Israel and the world. The first-century high priests were self-serving and faithful only to their own interests and the protection of their aristocratic status quo. The glorious character of Jesus makes Him a far superior High Priest to any before or after Him.

A SUPERIOR MINISTRY

Jesus was not only superior in His character but also in the nature of His ministry.

ETERNAL

God appointed Aaron's descendants to be a priesthood forever (Exodus 40:15), but no individual lived forever. The Jews in Jesus' day were terrified that the high priest would be struck dead by God on the Day of Atonement. It was also the custom to have a substitute ready to replace the chosen high priest in case he died (Yoma 1:1).

Believers need never fear that the high priestly ministry of Jesus will falter or fail. The author of Hebrews assures us that He always lives to make intercession for His people. "Hence also, He is able to save forever those who draw near to God through Him, since He always lives to make intercession for them" (Hebrews 7:25).

Jesus was not a priestly descendant of Aaron, nor a Levite. He was a priest in the same manner as Melchizedek, the priest-king of ancient Jerusalem. The eternality of His messianic priesthood rested upon His divine nature: "He has become a priest after the order of Melchizedek 'according to the power of an indestructible life' " (Hebrews 7:16); and "He [Jesus] . . . because He abides forever, holds His priesthood permanently" (Hebrews 7:24).

The ministry of Jesus was unlike that of His contemporary high priests who served only one-year terms. Although the priests before Herod's day were appointed to serve as high priests for their entire lives, they were still subject to sickness, incapacity, and death. The entire Levitical system was marred by human weakness. But the priesthood of Jesus is different; His ministry is everlasting and not subject to the frailties of the flesh. Believers can rest assured of His continual intercession on their behalf.

APPOINTED BY GOD

The ancient Levitical priests received their high priestly appointments through heredity. By the time of the second Temple, corrupt high priests connived and bribed their way to power. But Jesus was directly chosen and appointed by God. "And no one takes the honor to himself, but receives it when he is called by God, even as Aaron was. So also Christ did not glorify Himself so as to become a high priest, but He who said to Him, 'Thou art my Son, today I have begotten Thee' " (Hebrews 5:4-5).

Aaron himself was appointed by God to be the first Levitical high priest, but soon the priestly line was assumed by those whose character and testimony were far less worthy. Jesus, on the other hand, was chosen as high priest before the foundation of the world.

AT GOD'S RIGHT HAND

Jesus' contemporaries would serve a year and retire to become part of the Sadducean aristocracy. But He remained High Priest forever and was exalted to the right hand of the Father as vice-regent of heaven: "We have such a high priest, who has taken His seat at the right hand of the throne of the majesty in the heavens" (Hebrews 8:1). He is an exalted Priest and King, in the perfect position to continue His ministry to His people.

IN A BETTER SANCTUARY

The earthly Tabernacle was a marvelous sight, and the Temple of Herod one of the wonders of the world, yet both pale in comparison to the majesty of the heavenly sanctuary in which Jesus ministers (Hebrews 8:2). In that holy place there is no need for an Ark or a Mercy Seat, for His ministry of intercession is exercised in the presence of God.

OF A BETTER COVENANT

The prophet Jeremiah spoke of a New Covenant that would replace the Old: "Behold, days are coming," declares the Lord, "when I will make a new covenant with the house of Israel. . . . I will put My law within them, and on their heart I will write it; and I will be their God, and they shall be My people" (Jeremiah 31:31, 33).

Jesus Himself is the High Priest of this New Covenant, rendering the office of high priest for the Old Covenant no longer necessary: "But now He has obtained a more excellent ministry by as much as He is also the mediator of a better covenant, which has been enacted on better promises" (Hebrews 8:6). In this New Covenant, God inhabits the hearts of His people who are cleansed by Christ's blood and made fit to be holy vessels of God's Spirit. The New Covenant believer is a living Temple, bearing the Holy of Holies and the Shekinah presence in his heart.

A SUPERIOR SACRIFICE

Jesus is more than our messianic High Priest. He is the offering presented for the forgiveness of our sins. His sacrifice is superior in power as well as in simplicity.

IN POWER

The Old Covenant sacrifices were limited to the physical realm. They were offered by an earthly high priest on a temporary altar and were able to purify in only the most superficial manner. Animal sacrifices could never fully cleanse the worshipers' conscience. Offerings of bulls and goats could restore an Israelite to ritual purity within the nation but could not do anything for the individual's heart. This is poignantly captured by Isaac Watts:

> Not all the blood of beasts on Jewish altars slain
> Could give the guilty conscience peace, or wash
> away the stain;
> But Christ, the Heavenly Lamb, takes all our
> sins away,
> A sacrifice of nobler name and richer blood than
> they.[1]

1. F. F. Bruce, *The Epistle to the Hebrews* (Grand Rapids: Eerdmans, 1964), p. 205.

The Old Covenant sacrifices were unable to cleanse a man from within. Jesus said, "There is nothing outside the man which going into him can defile him; but the things which proceed out of the man are what defile the man" (Mark 7:15). British scholar F. F. Bruce writes, "But their pollution is removed from the conscience by the work of Christ, so that men and women, emancipated from inward bondage, can worship God in spirit and in truth. This is the 'perfection' which the ancient ceremonial was unable to achieve."[2]

What purpose then did the Old Testament sacrifices serve? After all, they were given to Israel by God Himself (Leviticus 1-7). The animal sacrifices taught the Israelites that the gruesome penalty for sin was death. They demonstrated that God was gracious in allowing substitutes to pay that terrible penalty. But the sacrificial system was a type, a foreshadowing, of God's ultimate sacrifice for sin, Jesus the Messiah (Galatians 3:24; Colossians 2:16-17; 1 John 2:2; 3:11).

The writer of Hebrews argues that the "blood of bulls and goats" never did "take away sins" (Hebrews 10:4) but only covered them for a time. "For the Law, since it has only a shadow of the good things to come and not the very form of things, can never by the same sacrifices year by year, which they offer continually, make perfect those who draw near" (Hebrews 10:1).

The Old Covenant faithful were forgiven in acknowledgment of their faith and in God's foreknowledge of Christ's work. Paul used the illustration of Abraham's justification by faith (Romans 4:3). But Abraham, who lived before the sacrificial system, and all faithful Israelites thereafter until Calvary, only had their sins passed over

2. Ibid.

and covered. The sins were never literally "taken away."
The apostle recognized this when he wrote: "Whom God
displayed publicly as a propitiation in His blood through
faith. This was to demonstrate His righteousness, because
in the forbearance of God He passed over the sins previously committed" (Romans 3:25).

Jesus' sacrifice satisfied the wrath of God and lifted
sin's obstruction to man's fellowship with Him. For only
through Jesus can believing men and women find reconciliation and peace with God.

The earthly high priest was commanded to sprinkle
blood on the Mercy Seat, the altar of incense, the sanctuary, and the altar itself. Even more so, the blood of Jesus
was powerful enough to cleanse the heavens of every remembrance of the believers' sin. "Therefore it was necessary for
the copies of the things in the heavens to be cleansed with
these, but the heavenly things themselves with better sacrifices than these" (Hebrews 9:23).

IN SIMPLICITY

The intricate sacrificial ritual revealed in Leviticus
had grown even more complicated by the time of Christ.
Yet more was accomplished in His one act of sacrifice on
Calvary than in all the Levitical rituals ever observed. The
author of Hebrews wrote, "He [Jesus] entered the holy
place once for all, having obtained eternal redemption"
(Hebrews 9:12; see also 10:10, 12).

He did not have to keep offering His sacrifice year after
year. The complete atonement of mankind's sins took
place in one act, on one day, in one moment on a hill outside Jerusalem. And, afterwards, Jesus took His seat "at the
right hand of the throne of the majesty in the heavens"
(Hebrews 8:1). His work was complete, atonement was
made, and He could rest from His labors.

The simplicity of His sacrifice is profound. All God ever wanted to accomplish in providing atonement for man was fulfilled in this one eternal action. The once-for-all sacrifice of Jesus is so simple in comparison to the elaborate ritual of the synagogue that Jewish people sometimes consider the gospel an all too easy path to faith. Yet it is consistent with God's nature to make His will known in an uncomplicated manner. There is only one way to the Father (John 14:6), and there is only one sacrifice for sin. We should stand amazed and marvel at the simplicity of God's truth. But it is simple only for us; that simple act cost God the life of His Son.

A Superior Access

The Temple was the religious and political focus of the nation. It was also a reminder to the average Israelite of what separated him from the presence of God (Hebrews 9:8-9), for he was never allowed to approach the sanctuary of the Lord. Levitical priests were able to enter the holy place, but they were never allowed into the Holy of Holies. That was the domain of the high priest alone, and he was permitted to enter within the veil only on the Day of Atonement. The individual Israelite was at the mercy of the high priest to bring him into the presence of God.

But the sacrifice of Jesus changed all that!

> Since therefore, brethren, we have confidence to enter the holy place by the blood of Jesus, by a new and living way which He inaugurated for us through the veil, that is, His flesh, and since we have a great priest over the house of God let us draw near with a sincere heart in full assurance of faith, having our hearts sprinkled clean from an evil conscience and our bodies washed with pure water. (Hebrews 10:19-22)

The author of Hebrews compares the flesh of Christ to the veil that divided the holy place from the Holy of Holies. We know from the gospels that when Jesus died this veil was rent (Mark 15:38; Matthew 27:51; Luke 23:45).

The New Covenant provides free access to the presence of God for all men as long as they enter through the merits of Christ's sacrifice. The Mosaic sacrifices could not purify the conscience, but the sacrifice of Christ relieved the worshiper of guilt and enabled him without fear to enter into the presence of God.

Believers who trust in the blood of Christ experience God's presence more than any high priest ever did. The ancient high priest could enter God's presence on one day each year, and then only with fear and trembling. Yet those of us who know Jesus can boldly enter His heavenly throne room and step into the glorious presence of God.

This communion with God is available to all who believe at all times because of the once-for-all sacrifice of Jesus at Calvary. One need not be a high priest, a Levite, or even a member of Abraham's race. Our faith relationship to the High Priest enables both Jews and Gentiles to approach the throne of God. The writer of Hebrews encourages us to "draw near with a sincere heart in full assurance of faith" because through His eternal sacrifice we have been cleansed from an evil conscience. Like the high priest, we have been washed, but not by ordinary water. We have been washed with pure water, the water of the Spirit, the water of the Word. Our hearts have been sprinkled clean, fulfilling the cleansing promise by Ezekiel (Ezekiel 36:25-27; Ephesians 5:26).

What a blessed opportunity for a Christian to have free access into the presence of God Himself. Ought we not to thank God for this great privilege through prayer and worship?

Praise be to God for His indescribable gift!

Part 3:

Sukkot

13
The Biblical Institution of Sukkot

The feast of Tabernacles completes the sacred festivals of the seventh month. In contrast to the somber tone of Trumpets and the Day of Atonement, the third feast of Tishri was a time of joy. Israel had passed through a season of repentance and redemption. The Lord wanted His people to enjoy the benefits of their renewed relationship with Him. The rigors of introspection and searching would now make way for the feast called "The Season of Our Rejoicing."

As Israel gathered leaves and branches, meticulously choosing the best and least blemished, as they laid the foundations of the flimsy booths, their every move reminded them of their time of wandering in the wilderness. It was only by the grace of God that they were granted the security of their present and permanent homes. As their nostrils filled with the pungent smell of myrtle and freshly cut palm, they remembered their days of uncertainty in the wilderness of Sinai. According to all natural laws, they should have perished, were it not for the Lord who guided their path, quenched their thirst, and satisfied their hunger above and beyond their needs. The delicate willow branches, a welcome sight growing along the banks of flowing brooks, filled their minds with thoughts of water springing from desert rocks.

For seven long days and nights the Israelites were to dwell in booths. The sensitive heart could not help but be overwhelmed with a feeling of poignancy, for certainly joy and plenty have not characterized the history of the Jewish people. Many a "season of joy" has been marred by prejudice, persecution, desecration, and bloodshed.

Such calamities were graphically predicted by the prophet Moses when he declared to the people: "If you will diligently obey the Lord your God . . . all these blessings shall come upon you . . . if you will not obey the Lord your God . . . all these curses shall come upon you" (Deuteronomy 28:1-2, 15; see vv. 16-68 and Leviticus 26:14-39).

Moses gave Israel the choice between obedience and disobedience, a life of joy and plenty or curses and desolation. If Israel chose disobedience, they would have no cause for rejoicing, nor would they care to celebrate the feast in gratitude to the God of joy!

The Names of the Feast

The many names for the feast of Booths attest to its prominent role in the Hebrew calendar. As each facet in a diamond yields a new prism of colors, the names of the feast serve as windows into the world of the festival.

THE FEAST OF BOOTHS

The name "The Feast of Booths" (Hebrew, *Sukkot*)[1] recalls the commandment in Leviticus: "You shall live in booths for seven days . . . so that your generations may know that I had the sons of Israel live in booths when I brought them out from the land of Egypt. I am the Lord your God" (Leviticus 23:42-43).

---

1. Used in Leviticus 23:34; Deuteronomy 16:13, 16; 31:10; 2 Chronicles 8:13; Ezra 3:4; Zechariah 14:16, 18-19.

The impermanent, vulnerable, leafy shelters were to remind the Israelites of God's faithfulness during their forty years of wandering in the desert. The booths symbolized man's need to depend on God for His provision of food, water, and shelter. This is true in the spiritual realm as well, for without the provision of His presence and power, all men would be left naked and destitute. Our world is a spiritual desert, scorching the soul without the Holy One's life-giving intervention on our behalf.

In ancient Israel, booths were in common use throughout the land. The Hebrew word *sukkah* originally meant "woven." Temporary shelters were woven together from branches and leaves to protect livestock (Genesis 33:17), to provide resting places for warriors during battle (2 Samuel 11:11), to shelter watchers in the vineyard (Isaiah 1:8), and to protect the people from the incessant heat of the merciless Middle-Eastern sun. During harvest time, Israelite fields were dotted with such booths, woven hastily together as temporary homes for the harvesters.

THE FEAST OF INGATHERING

The command to build booths and dwell in them coincided annually with Israel's final harvest, and so the name "Feast of Ingathering" was used for the holiday as well. In Leviticus 23:34 we read that the feast was to begin on the fifteenth day of the seventh month, but in other portions of Scripture the beginning point for the feast is less definite. For example, in Exodus 23:16 the celebration is to start "at the end of the year when you gather in the fruit of your labors from the field." In the previous verse where God ordains the celebration of Passover, He makes mention of the "appointed time in the month Abib" (Exodus 23:15). So it is interesting that the fifteenth of Tishri is not mentioned in this verse. In Deuteronomy 16:13 Moses again leaves out the date: "You shall celebrate the Feast of Booths seven days after you have gathered in from your threshing floor and your wine vat."

We are not certain why the date of the feast, which is certainly significant, is not mentioned in these two passages. Perhaps the reason is simply that the emphasis of the passage is on the relationship of the holiday to the final gathering of crops in the fall. Some would suggest that the Exodus passage reflects an earlier tradition that set a date for the feast of Tabernacles whenever the harvest was complete. This is an unacceptable solution because Leviticus 23 clearly states that the feast was to begin on the fifteenth of Tishri. If the "Torah" was given by God at Mount Sinai, it would be unreasonable to suggest that the Exodus passage was written before Leviticus. A better solution might simply involve a matter of emphasis. The Exodus and Deuteronomy passages emphasize the relationship of Tabernacles to the ingathering of the crops, whereas the institution of the feast in Leviticus 23 and Numbers 29:12-38 depicts the feast in its broadest and most panoramic sense.

Ancient Israel's economy was agrarian. There was no industry; there were no office buildings. Extensive foreign trade had not yet been established by the young nation. The focal point of daily life revolved around the crops the people needed for sustenance. The seasons guided Israel's activities—the rain decreed their sustenance from year to year. Without rain, Israel, in its arid Middle-Eastern location, was as much in peril of famine as Egypt had been in the time of Joseph.

In our day of international trade and relief organizations, it is difficult to grasp the impact that a year with scant rainfall would have upon a fledgling nation. If there is a food shortage today, we have many alternative sources for supplies. However, that was not so for the Hebrews. Each season's plentiful harvest brought a renewed sense of relief and thankfulness that children would not go hungry, for God had once more provided for His people.

THE SEASON OF OUR JOY

Perhaps this is why the feast of Ingathering also came to be called "The Season of Our Joy." The agricultural year was at an end, the crops were gathered into the storehouses. The work was done, the harvest was over; and the joy that was unleashed at the end of a long, hard labor found the perfect outlet for expression. God gave Israel seven festival days to set aside all worldly cares and thank and praise Him who had provided in abundance.

THE FEAST

The impact of the holiday upon the Israelites was so significant that the feast of Booths came to be known as the "feast of the Lord," or more familiarly, "the feast." The Hebrew word *hag* comes from the root meaning "to dance or to be joyous" and applies exclusively to the three festivals of Passover, Pentecost, and Tabernacles, in which all males were to appear before the Lord in the sanctuary. There was no need to ask a fellow Jew what he meant by "the feast," just as there is no need today to ask a fellow countryman what he means by "the flag." This most loved of all holidays, this season of our joy, this final feast in the annual cycle, was indeed a high point in the life of the Israelites. It was *the* feast!

Two other names for the feast bear a short note of explanation. In "the feast of Sukkot," Sukkot is merely the original Hebrew term for "booths." Likewise, in "the feast of Tabernacles," a well-known name in non-Jewish circles, Tabernacles is a transliteration from the Vulgate of the Latin word *tabernacula*. A tabernacle always alludes to that which is temporary; whether that be the Holy Tabernacle that housed the Shekinah until the building of the more permanent Temple or the booths that housed the Israelites until they settled and built stone dwellings in the land of promise.

THE COMMANDED OBSERVANCES

What exactly were the Jewish people commanded to do during those seven days? The detailed instructions were given at Mount Sinai:

> Again the Lord spoke to Moses, saying, "Speak to the sons of Israel, saying, 'On the fifteenth of this seventh month is the Feast of Booths for seven days to the Lord.
>
> 'On the first day is a holy convocation; you shall do no laborious work of any kind.
>
> 'For seven days you shall present an offering by fire to the Lord. On the eighth day you shall have a holy convocation and present an offering by fire to the Lord; it is an assembly. You shall do no laborious work.
>
> 'On exactly the fifteenth day of the seventh month, when you have gathered in the crops of the land, you shall celebrate the feast of the Lord for seven days, with a rest on the first day and a rest on the eighth day.
>
> 'Now on the first day you shall take for yourselves the foliage of beautiful trees, palm branches and boughs of leafy trees and willows of the brook; and you shall rejoice before the Lord your God for seven days.
>
> 'You shall thus celebrate it as a feast to the Lord for seven days in the year. It shall be a perpetual statute throughout your generations; you shall celebrate it in the seventh month.
>
> 'You shall live in booths for seven days; all the native-born in Israel shall live in booths, so that your generations may know that I had the sons of Israel live in booths when I brought them out from the land of Egypt. I am the Lord your God.' " (Leviticus 23:33-36; 39-43)

The feast of Booths was to be set apart from the rest of the Hebrew year. As a master composer enhances his symphonies with rests to prepare the listener's ears for the theme, so the God of all harmony orchestrated this season of joy. After the labor of the harvest came a pause—the first day of Sukkot, a holy convocation, a time to cease working and gather in worship. The term that means to cease working is not as strong as the one used in connection with the Sabbath and the Day of Atonement. Here, it simply means that the Israelites should not perform their occupational tasks for the two days of holy convocation; but they were not required to endure the heavier restrictions required on the Day of Atonement and the Sabbath.

Here was a joyful interlude—the middle days of the feast—a time of great rejoicing as God was remembered and praised for His sustaining power. And then, silence—once more a holy convocation to draw to an end this exuberant season and bring to focus the events of the past week. And after the silence, the gentle, unassuming melody of life continued as before. The rhythmical arrangement of Sukkot was no accident but a symphonic creation of the Master Composer of the universe.

THE BUILDING OF BOOTHS

The Israelites were to gather bunches of boughs and build leafy booths in which to dwell for seven days. Living in booths was a reminder not of an unsettled time in the wilderness but of the sustenance, care, and protection given by God in the desert of Sinai. The prophet Isaiah writes, "And there will be a shelter to give shade from the heat by day, and refuge and protection from the storm and rain" (Isaiah 4:6). The prophet is speaking of how God will preserve the faithful remnant of Israel during the time of Jacob's trouble, but it does seem clear that Isaiah viewed the original pillar of fire as some kind of tabernacle.

The foliage of the booth reminded the Israelites of their humble origins in the desert; of the way God cared for them, teaching them to appreciate the fruitful heritage they were to receive in the land. The booth was a reminder that God would shelter His people and give them food as long as they were obedient to Him.[2]

There is some question as to whether the branches spoken of in this passage were to be used as building materials for the booths or as part of a separate, joyful wave-offering. This has been extensively discussed throughout Jewish history, and elaborate laws and rituals have developed espousing the latter belief.

A COMMAND TO REJOICE

As on Pentecost, the Israelites were *commanded* to rejoice during the feast. Moses wrote:

> You shall celebrate the Feast of Booths seven days after you have gathered in from your threshing floor and your wine vat; and you shall rejoice in your feast, you and your son and your daughter and your male and female servants and the Levite and the stranger and the orphan and the widow who are in your towns. (Deuteronomy 16:13-14)

In contrast to Yom Kippur and Rosh Hashanah, Sukkot was a time of rejoicing. This festive atmosphere resulted from the Hebrews' thankfulness for the final harvest. We see that in Deuteronomy 16:15, where the Lord says, "Seven days you shall celebrate a feast to the Lord your God in the place which the Lord chooses, because the Lord your God will bless you in all your produce and in all the work of your hands, so that you shall be *altogether joyful*" (italics added).

Is it any wonder that the rabbis gave the name *Zeman Simhatenu* ("the season of our joy") to the feast? The Is-

2. Keil and Delitzsch, vol. 1, p. 723.

raelites were to rejoice in God's provision for their daily bread *and* their spiritual lives.

There is yet one more explanation for the commandment to rejoice at the feast of Tabernacles. If the theme of Rosh Hashanah is repentance, and the theme of Yom Kippur is redemption, then most naturally the theme of Sukkot is rejoicing in God's forgiveness. The gathering of the year's final harvest was a confirmation of God's blessing upon the Jewish people for their obedience to His law. Salvation and obedience to God always leads to joy.

THE SACRIFICES

The order of sacrifices on Sukkot is spelled out in minute detail in the book of Numbers. Never before had so many sacrifices been required of Israel on any one day. The vast numbers of sacrifices were commensurate with Israel's depth of thanksgiving for a bountiful harvest.

A fascinating and mysterious pattern emerges from the seemingly endless list of sacrifices. No matter how the offerings are grouped or counted, their number always remains divisible by the number seven. During the week are offered 70 bullocks, 14 rams, and 98 lambs—altogether 182 sacrifices (26 x 7), to which must be added 336 (48 x 7) tenths of ephahs of flour for the meal offering. As compared with the feast of Unleavened Bread, the number of rams and lambs is double, whereas that of the bullocks is fivefold (14 during the Passover week, 5 x 14 during that of Tabernacles).

It was no coincidence that this seven-day holiday, which took place in the height of the seventh month, had the perfect number, seven, imprinted on its sacrifices. It was by divine design that the final holiday of the Jewish religious year bore on its sacrifices the seal of God's perfect approval.

A question arises as to the nature of the *atzeret*, or the eighth day of the feast. Several scholars think that the eighth day does not belong to the feast of Tabernacles but rather serves as a conclusion and final note to all the feasts mentioned in Leviticus 23. Keil and Delitzsch write:

> The atzeret as the eighth day did not strictly belong to the feast of Tabernacles, which was only to last seven days; and it was distinguished, moreover from these seven days by a smaller number of offerings (Numbers 29:35ff). The eighth day was rather the solemn close of the whole circle of yearly feasts, and therefore was appended to the close of the last of these feasts as the eighth day of the feast itself (see Numbers 28ff).[3]

Like Keil and Delitzsch, Theodore Gaster views the atzeret as distinct from Sukkot. He notes that the word *atzeret* comes from a root that means "restrained."[4] It is possible that the day of atzeret originally denoted a day of abstinence and austerity that "marked the end of the reaping and the real beginning of the new agricultural cycle."

The fact that sacrificial requirements were profoundly reduced for the eighth day, the atzeret, is another reason to believe that it is to be viewed as a distinct festival and not necessarily an integral part of Sukkot.

Every year at the appointed season, the feast of Tabernacles was to be celebrated, reminding Israel of God's provision in the wilderness and of His continuing sustenance now. Yet the celebration of Sukkot was soon abandoned as Israel settled into the land of Canaan. The feast fell by the wayside as the people's fervent promises at Mount Sinai were forgotten.

3. Ibid., p. 720.
4. Theodore Gaster, *Festivals of the Jewish Year* (New York: William Morrow, 1953), p. 98.

14
The Observance of Sukkot in Biblical Times

From the heights of the fiery mountain, where the chosen nation declared her allegiance to the one true God and His precepts, Israel tumbled down a steep precipice of apathy. The dedication and good intentions of the Israelites dissipated. The festivals became memories. The glowing declaration "All that the Lord hath said will we do, and be obedient" (Exodus 24:7) was an expression of enthusiasm that faded. Nehemiah, centuries later, reflected upon Hebrew history and wrote, "The sons of Israel had indeed not done so [observed the feast of Tabernacles] from the days of Joshua the son of Nun to that day" (Nehemiah 8:17).

The most joyous of thanksgiving feasts was scarcely celebrated in Israel, for the people had neglected their source of sustenance—their Maker.

SOLOMON'S DEDICATION OF THE TEMPLE

There were moments when faithful men attempted to reinstitute the festival. Nehemiah 8:17 requires careful interpretation on this issue, because the feast may have been celebrated in 1 Kings 8 at the time of the dedication of Solomon's Temple and at the time of Jeroboam I. Keil and Delitzsch believe that Nehemiah 8:17 has a direct reference to the act of living in booths: the Israelites celebrated the feast with holy convocation and sacrifice but failed to observe the command to "dwell in booths."[1] That may be so, but in light of biblical history, it does seem that the feast was only rarely observed.

In fact, under the leadership of King Solomon the feast of Booths seems to have been chosen above all other feasts for the grand occasion of the dedication of the Temple. We cannot say conclusively that the feast of Sukkot was actually celebrated by Solomon, since we do not read of booths being erected. But it appears from this account that Solomon did choose the days of Sukkot to dedicate the Temple. Scripture does not tell us in what year the Temple was dedicated.

"And all the men of Israel assembled themselves to King Solomon at the feast in the month Ethanim, which is the seventh month."[2] Gesenius, the great Hebrew linguist of the nineteenth century, tells us that the name *Ethanim* may well be taken from a word meaning "the month of the flowing brooks." Tishri is called Ethanim because the seventh month usually marked the beginning of the rainy season in ancient Israel (1 Kings 8:2).

Some say that Solomon chose the feast because of the great number of pilgrims that came to Jerusalem for its celebration. But it would seem that he chose Sukkot because its themes were so appropriate for the event.

For twenty long years Solomon's people labored, with intricate plans and precious materials, to fulfill the dream of King David and build a house for the Lord. As Solomon gazed upon this magnificent symbol of God's presence, his heart overflowed with gratitude. What more fitting time to express his delight than at the feast of Tabernacles, the supreme season of joy and thanksgiving? From all corners of

1. Keil and Delitzsch, vol. 3, p. 71.
2. Ibid., vol. 2, p. 609.

the land, Solomon called his people to come and celebrate. A festival of this magnitude had never before been seen in Israel—so many sheep and oxen were sacrificed that they could not be counted.

Solomon stood before the altar, and spreading his hands towards heaven he bared his soul in prayer. He blessed the Lord God of Israel, praised Him for His faithfulness in keeping His covenant and fulfilling the promise to David. Solomon recognized that God is omnipresent. Like David, Solomon knew that the presence of God could not be limited by any mere human structure (see Psalm 139). He prayed, "But will God indeed dwell on the earth? Behold, heaven and the highest heaven cannot contain Thee, how much less this house which I have built!" (1 Kings 8:27).

The Temple was a temporary dwelling for the presence of God. His desire was to fill the whole earth with the glory of His presence (Numbers 14:21; Isaiah 6:3). This is so beautifully expressed by Solomon himself in Psalm 72:19: "Blessed be the Lord God, the God of Israel, who alone works wonders. And blessed be His glorious name forever; and may the whole earth be filled with His glory. Amen, and amen."

The remainder of Solomon's prayer may also have had the feast of Sukkot in mind, for the festival was conditioned upon the repentance and faithfulness of God's people. The harvest would come to fruition only as Israel obeyed the covenant and received the blessing of God.

> When the heavens are shut up and there is no rain, because they have sinned against Thee, and they pray toward this place and confess Thy name and turn from their sin when Thou dost afflict them, then hear Thou in heaven and forgive the sin of Thy servants and of Thy people Israel, indeed teach them the good way in which they should walk. And send rain on Thy land, which

Thou hast given Thy people for an inheritance. (1 Kings 8:35-36)

It was God's desire that Israel be a "light to the nations" and that the Temple be their beacon. That is why the Temple was called "a house of prayer for all the peoples" (Isaiah 56:7). Solomon pleaded with the Lord to have mercy upon those Gentiles who turn to the God of Israel.

Also concerning the foreigner who is not of Thy people Israel, when he comes from a far country for Thy name's sake (for they will hear of Thy great name and Thy mighty hand, and of Thine outstretched arm); when he comes and prays toward this house, hear Thou in heaven Thy dwelling place, and do according to all for which the foreigner calls to Thee, in order that all the peoples of the earth may know Thy name. (1 Kings 8:41-43)

The theme of God's concern for the heathen nations is woven into the core of Sukkot. Solomon reflected on the end of the final harvest, a time of rest and thanksgiving, and thanked his God, who gave "rest to His people Israel, according to all that He promised" (1 Kings 8:56).

King Solomon was so zealous in his celebration of the feast that after the prayer he once again offered sacrifices to the Lord. This time, however, they *could* be counted: 22,000 oxen and 120,000 sheep. Considering the size of this offering, one cannot help but wonder at the size of the earlier sacrifice, which the Scriptures said "could not be counted or numbered" (1 Kings 8:5).

Solomon and all Israel celebrated the feast of Tabernacles for more than the required seven days. Their gratitude and joy compelled them to extend the feast yet another week (1 Kings 8:65). And after the last day, when the people were dismissed, "they went to their tents joyful and glad of heart for all the goodness that the Lord had shown to David His servant and to Israel His people" (1 Kings 8:66).

THE PROPHETIC BOOKS

Psalms, the song book of the Jewish people, makes reference to the feast (see Psalms 42, 81), as do the prophets of Israel (see Zechariah 14:16-19). An unusual allusion to the feast of Tabernacles is found in Hosea 9, a passage describing God's judgment of the Northern Kingdom. The prophet chided Israel, saying, "What will you do on the day of the appointed festival and on the day of the feast of the Lord?" (v. 5). Hosea implied that Israel would not have anything to celebrate because they would be receiving God's wrath rather than His blessing. Disobedience to the law brought judgment upon the nation. They had no crops to gather and no joy to inspire celebration (Leviticus 26; Deuteronomy 28). Israel could enjoy the feast of Booths only if God blessed their harvest, and the harvest was given as a result of their obedience.

AFTER THE EXILE

Sukkot was celebrated by the exiles returning from the Babylonian captivity:

> Now when the seventh month came, and the sons of Israel were in the cities, the people gathered together as one man to Jerusalem.
>
> Then Jeshua the son of Jozadak and his brothers the priests, and Zerubbabel the son of Shealtiel, and his brothers arose and built the altar of the God of Israel, to offer burnt offerings on it, as it is written in the law of Moses, the man of God.
>
> So they set up the altar on its foundation, for they were terrified because of the peoples of the lands; and they offered burnt offerings on it to the Lord, burnt offerings morning and evening.

> And they celebrated the feast of Booths, as it is written, and offered the fixed number of burnt offerings daily, according to the ordinance, as each day required. (Ezra 3:1-4)

The remnant, returning with gladness in their hearts, yearned to celebrate the feast of Tabernacles. Hastily, they erected an altar and began to sacrifice, to pour out their thankfulness to God.

It is of this scene that Nehemiah recounted:

> And they found written in the law how the Lord had commanded through Moses that the sons of Israel should live in booths during the feast of the seventh month.
>
> So they proclaimed and circulated a proclamation in all their cities and in Jerusalem, saying, "Go out to the hills, and bring olive branches, and wild olive branches, myrtle branches, palm branches, and branches of other leafy trees, to make booths, as it is written." (Nehemiah 8:14-15)

The people had forgotten the feast of Tabernacles in the Babylonian captivity. Now, as Ezra read Moses' words, they responded with fervency. Thousands upon thousands of Israelites set out to gather myrtle, palm, and olive branches. On their roofs, in their courts, even in the courts of the house of God, tents of foliage were erected. "And the entire assembly of those who had returned from the captivity made booths and lived in them. The sons of Israel had indeed not done so from the days of Joshua the son of Nun to that day. And there was great rejoicing" (Nehemiah 8:17).

The booths built in the courts of the house of God were probably built by the Levites for their personal use. There were also booths built in two other public places: at the Water Gate and at the Gate of Ephraim for the pilgrims who left their homes and traveled up to Jerusalem in order to celebrate.

Every letter of the law was followed, from the holy convocations, to the building of the tents, to the intricate and mysterious sacrifices throughout the feast's seven days. The people's eagerness to thank their God could not be contained.

INTERTESTAMENTAL PERIOD

The apocryphal book of Jubilees mentions the feast of Booths, speculating that it originated with Abraham:

> For it is ordained forever regarding Israel that they should celebrate it and dwell in booths and set wreaths upon their heads and take leafy boughs and willows from the brook. And Abraham took branches of palm trees and the fruit of good trees, and every day going around the altar with the branches seven times in the morning, he praised and gave thanks to his God for all things in joy. (Jubilees 16:20-31; also mentioned in Jubilees 32:4-9)

The celebration of Sukkot is mentioned in the Scriptures on two high points in Israel's history: the dedication of the Temple and the return from the Babylonian captivity. Scripture's relative silence about the feast's observance in biblical times is unfortunate evidence that Israel had low points in their history as well. The saga of Israel's history is marked by disobedience and judgment rather than enjoyment of God's harvest blessings in the land. The joy of Sukkot was linked to Israel's faithful obedience to God's law, but Israel's disobedience kept them from enjoying God and celebrating this feast.

By the time of Christ, though, Tabernacles was regularly observed and formed the backdrop for some of the most profound statements of Jesus the Messiah, who would indeed be God dwelling among men (John 1:14).

15

Sukkot in the Time of Christ

Jerusalem must have been magnificent during the month of Tishri—each festival was more spectacular than the last. But the cycle reached its high point during the celebration of Sukkot.

The Jewish people were not required to go up to Jerusalem for the feast of Trumpets or the Day of Atonement, but they *were* required to do so for Sukkot. Jerusalem was dotted with thousands of lean-tos, their thatched roofs and wooden foundations scattered throughout. Jerusalem could not possibly have held the number of booths needed to house the pilgrims of Sukkot. The buzz of activity was at a high pitch—there was not much time after Yom Kippur to scour the terrain for the choicest of materials with which to build the booths.

Not only would booths have to be prepared, but sacrificial animals would have to be herded into Jerusalem to provide the large number of sacrifices necessary for each day of the feast. More animals were sacrificed during the week of Sukkot than during any other time of the Jewish year. The Temple area must have been inundated with bulls, goats, and lambs.

Jerusalem was more crowded during this holiday than at any other time of the year. Alfred Edersheim envisions the scene:

On the day before the Feast of Tabernacles—the 14th of
Tishri—the festive pilgrims had all arrived in Jerusalem.
The booths on the roofs, in the courtyards, in streets and
squares, as well as roads and gardens, within a Sabbath
day's journey must have given the city and neighbor-
hood an unusually picturesque appearance. The preparation of all that was needed for the festival—purification, the care of the offerings that each would bring, and
friendly communications between those who were to be
invited to the sacrificial meal—no doubt sufficiently oc-
cupied their time. When the early autumn evening set
in, the blast of the priests' trumpets on the Temple mount
announced to Israel the advent of the Feast.[1]

Most of the information we have about the celebration
of Tabernacles in the time of Christ comes from the Mishna and the New Testament. The Jewish customs of Tabernacles in the time of Christ must be understood in order to
fully appreciate the way Jesus used the event to proclaim
His message. The feast of Sukkot set a magnificent stage for
the preaching of Christ.

THE CEREMONY OF THE WATER DRAWING

The Mishna describes a major ceremony of Sukkot,
one of fairly late origin, which was not part of the biblical
celebration of the feast. The ritual is called the ceremony
of the water drawing, in Hebrew, *Nissuch Ha-Mayim,* and
is rooted in the agricultural character of the feast. Rain is
essential to the growing of crops, and Israel, an arid land,
prized rain greatly as a blessing from God. The Israelites,
depending upon God for rain, developed a ceremony in
which they called upon their Creator to provide heavenly
waters for their crops.

1. Edersheim, p.277.

Sukkot was also the changing point of the seasons, closing the agricultural or working year. It marked the change of seasons with the approach of rain. Rain was a prominent feature in the celebration of the feast of Sukkot.

The water-drawing ceremony was a joyous occasion, replete with grand activity and high drama. It began with an especially assigned Levitical priest descending to the pool of Siloam. He was accompanied by a throng of faithful worshipers and a band of liturgical flutists whose lilting music enhanced the wonder of the ceremony. When the Levitical priest arrived at the pool of Siloam, he filled a special golden pitcher with water. The crowd then returned to the Temple through the Water Gate, which obtained its name from the ceremony. As the priest arrived, the trumpets—rams' horns similar to the ones used on Rosh Hashanah—were sounded. The Mishna specified that there should first be a prolonged blast and then a quavering note, then again a prolonged blast of the Temple trumpet.

The priest entered the Temple area and went directly to the southern side of the great altar. There, he placed two magnificent silver basins on the southwest corner of the altar. These two bowls were slightly different from one another. The wide-mouthed bowl on the eastern side was used to receive the wine of the drink offering. The western basin was somewhat narrower, and into it was poured the water from the pool of Siloam. As soon as the priest poured the water into the basin, the people surrounding the altar would shout, "Raise thy hand. Raise thy hand!" The crowd was insistent on making sure the priest had indeed poured the water and poured it properly. This tradition goes back to approximately 95 B.C. when Alexander Jannaeus, one of the Maccabean priest kings, wickedly poured the festival water on the ground rather than upon the altar. At that point, according to tradition, the crowd carrying both lulav (branches) and etrog (fruit) began pelting him with their etrogs. The event escalated into a massacre, and legend says that no less than six thousand Jews were killed in the Temple (Sukkah 9).[2]

The liturgical flutists kept playing while the water was poured into the basin, except on the Sabbath and on the first day of the feast when flute playing was not allowed (Sukkah 5:1). The flutists were joined by a choir of Israelites chanting the words of the Psalm 118, "O Lord, do save, we beseech Thee; O Lord, we beseech Thee, do send prosperity!" (Psalm 118:25). As these words were repeated, the worshipers shook palm branches towards the altar until all the water was poured. (It is remarkable that when the multitude from Jerusalem came out to meet Jesus, they cut down branches from trees and tossed them in His path. The multitude then chanted the next verse of the psalm, "Hosanna to the Son of David; blessed is He who comes in the name of the Lord; hosanna in the highest!" [Matthew 21:9]. This may have been an allusion to this ceremony of the feast of Tabernacles, although there is a tradition of shaking palm branches at Passover as well.)

The ceremony of the water drawing held a significance much deeper than its agricultural implications. The rain represented the Holy Spirit, and the water drawing pointed to that day when, according to the prophet Joel, God would rain His Spirit upon the Israelites (Joel 2:28). The prayer of every worshiper was, "May God send His Spirit upon us *now.*" In the Talmud we read, "Why is the name of it called the drawing out of water? Because of the pouring out of the Holy Spirit, according to what is said: 'With joy shall ye draw out of the wells of salvation' "(Isaiah 12:3).[3]

These same rabbinical authorities believed joy to signal the presence of God's Spirit. Joy is the all-pervasive

2. Ibid., p. 279.
3. Ibid., p. 280.

theme of the feast of Tabernacles. The Mishna says, "Anyone who has not witnessed the rejoicing of the libation water-well has never seen rejoicing in his life" (Sukkah 5:1).

The drama of the water drawing ceremony took on a new dimension of meaning when Jesus attended the feast of Tabernacles. It was the seventh day of the feast, *Hoshana Rabbah*, which literally means "the Great Hosanna," and was called the great day of the feast. The festival activities were different that day. On each of the six previous days, the priests circled the altar in procession, singing, "O Lord, do save, we beseech Thee; O Lord, we beseech thee, do send prosperity!" (Psalm 118:25). On the seventh day of the feast, though, they circled the altar seven times. That is why the day is called Hoshana Rabbah, as the cry *Hosheanah* ("save now") was repeated seven times.

There is some discussion as to whether or not Jesus' statement in John 7:37-39 took place on the seventh day of the feast, Hoshana Rabbah, or on the eighth day, the Atzeret. The older commentators, including Alford and Lange, suggest that Jesus' comments on the Holy Spirit were pronounced on the eighth day.[4]

The debates over a seventh or eighth day setting for the statements of Jesus in John 7:37-39 hinge on two matters. First, there is the question of the relationship of the Atzeret to the feast of Tabernacles. If the eighth day, the Atzeret, is in fact an intrinsic part of Tabernacles rather than the culmination of the holidays of Tishri, then that would lend credence to the view that the great day of the feast was the eighth day. In ancient sources, the holiday is

4. John Peter Lange, "The Gospel According to John," *Lange's Commentary on the Holy Scriptures: Critical, Doctrinal and Homiletical,* trans. and ed. Phillip Schaff, reprint (Grand Rapids: Zondervan, 1871), p. 256.

said to be an eight-day holiday (2 Maccabees 10:6; Josephus *Antiquities* 3.10.4).

There is also a question as to whether or not the water-drawing ceremony continued on the eighth day of the feast. The common teaching of the Mishna is that the water drawing did not continue on the eighth day, and only Rabbi Judah, issuing a minority opinion, asserted that it did. Since the Mishna is our major source for understanding these matters, it would seem that the water drawing did not take place on the eighth day (Sukkah). If the opinion is accepted that the water-drawing ceremony did not take place on the eighth day, some would still attribute the statement in John 7:37-39 to the eighth day, claiming that Jesus was merely alluding to the ceremony of the water drawing. It appears, though, that the seventh day, Hoshana Rabbah, was the natural setting for the declarations of Jesus at the festival.

On this day, the number of bullocks offered on the altar was reduced to seven, telling us that the cycle of feasts was complete. It was the last day the Israelites would sleep in booths. One can only imagine the intensity of worship reached by the Israelites on this great seventh day of the feast.

The city of Jerusalem was filled to capacity. The myriad pilgrims who came from throughout the Diaspora pressed against one another. Once again the priest went to the pool of Siloam with his entourage of fellow worshipers and liturgical flutists. He filled the sacred vessels and returned to the altar amidst the music of the flutes, the chants of the Levitical choir, and the haunting blasts of the shofar.

In the presence of thousands of worshipers, a young itinerant rabbi from Nazareth proclaimed a message that would quench the thirst of the most thirsty soul.

> Now on the last day, the great day of the feast, Jesus stood and cried out, saying, "If any man is thirsty, let

him come to me and drink. He who believes in me, as the Scriptures said, 'from his innermost being shall flow rivers of living water.' " But this He spoke of the Spirit, whom those who believed in Him were to receive, for the Spirit was not yet given because Jesus was not yet glorified. (John 7:37-39)

Jesus invited the whole congregation of Israel to come and drink of living water, just as He had previously extended a similar invitation to the woman at the well. Water maintains human life and causes crops to grow. It is easy to see how water became a symbol of life in a land as arid as Israel. Yet the invitation was not to those who merely thirst for water but rather to those who hunger and thirst for righteousness, whose hearts pant after God as a deer pants after water (Psalm 42:1). The water that Jesus offers is totally satisfying (John 4:13) and produces a well of living waters springing up into everlasting life (John 7:38). What was presented as a spring to the woman at the well is now pictured as a flowing river.

The act of drinking refers to believing in Christ. "If any man is thirsty, let him come to Me and drink" (John 7:37) is parallel to "He who believes in Me . . . from his innermost being shall flow rivers of living water" (John 7:38). To come to Jesus and drink is to believe in Him as the Savior and source of eternal life. The bubbling inner spring and the thundering flow of living water are references to the Holy Spirit and His ministry of indwelling all who believe (John 14:17; 1 Corinthians 12:13).

Jesus introduced the statement "From his innermost being shall flow rivers of living water" by using the phrase "as the Scripture said." There is no exact statement like this in the Old Testament, but numerous Scriptures link the symbol of water with the outpouring of the Holy Spirit.

The prophet Isaiah wrote, "For I will pour out water on the thirsty land and streams on the ground; I will pour out

My Spirit on your offspring and My blessing on your descendants" (Isaiah 44:3). Isaiah parallels the "thirsty land" with the future generations of Israel and links water with the Holy Spirit. The similarity to Jesus' words is unmistakable.

The idea of living waters was not foreign to Jesus' listeners. Zechariah spoke of life-giving messianic streams: "And it will come about in that day that living waters will flow out of Jerusalem, half of them toward the eastern sea and the other half toward the western sea; it will be in summer as well as in winter" (Zechariah 14:8).

One might also include Joel 2:23, Zechariah 13:1, and a number of other passages that either link together or allude to a relationship between water and the pouring out of the Holy Spirit. The majority of these Old Testament passages point to God's activity in the end times. The prophet Ezekiel wrote:

> For I will take you from the nations, gather you from all the lands, and bring you into your own land. Then I will sprinkle clean water on you, and you will be clean; I will cleanse you from all your filthiness and from all your idols. Moreover I will give you a new heart and put a new spirit within you; I will remove the heart of stone from your flesh and give you a heart of flesh. And I will put my Spirit within you and cause you to walk in my statutes and you will be careful to observe my ordinances. (Ezekiel 36:24-27)

The prophet combined thoughts of living water, the pouring out of the Spirit, messianic times, and the final redemption of the Jewish people. That is why Jesus assumed that Nicodemus would understand when He said, "Truly, truly I say to you, unless one is born of water and the Spirit he cannot enter into the kingdom of God" (John 3:5). Nicodemus, the ruler of the Jews, should have thought of Ezekiel's words after being spiritually jarred by this statement of Jesus.

What, then, was Jesus offering to the Jewish people on the feast of Tabernacles? He was offering life and redemption. He was also announcing to the pilgrims at the feast that His coming ushered in the promised messianic age—a time of restoration and forgiveness for the Jewish people. And the way to enjoy the salvation of the new age is to drink the living water offered by Jesus.

This spectacular invitation of Jesus on Hoshana Rabbah was not His first declaration at the feast of Tabernacles. He had already been preaching during the feast: "But when it was now the midst of the feast Jesus went up into the temple, and began to teach" (John 7:14). This was a daring and courageous step, for earlier He had been "unwilling to walk in Judea, because the Jews were seeking to kill Him" (John 7:1).

Is it possible that the Jewish multitudes recognized, in the coming of Jesus, God's messianic outpouring of His Holy Spirit through the presence of the anointed One, and through Him the fulfillment of their joy?

Yet His statements at the feast continued to fan the flames of controversy. Some were amazed at His teaching (John 7:14-15); others accused Him of having a demon (John 7:20). Some worshipers even speculated whether the Jewish rulers really knew that He was the Christ: "The rulers do not really know that this is the Christ, do they?" (John 7:26). After all, He was teaching, and no one was stopping Him.

Jesus stayed away from public attention for a few days. He waited for the day of the Great Hosanna to announce that He was the source of blessing and refreshment God would send in the latter days—and that both Jews and Gentiles must drink of Him to find everlasting life.

His statements caused a stir among the pilgrims. Some were saying that He was the "Prophet" (John 7:40), whereas others again wanted to seize Him (John 7:44). The controversy grew so severe that the Pharisees began arguing among themselves. Nicodemus, probably a secret believer at this time, finally put a stop to the conversation by saying, "Our Law does not judge a man, unless it first hears from him and knows what he is doing, does it?" (John 7:51). He said this at great personal risk, as he was almost accused of being a follower of Jesus. But His statements had their designed effect, and the controversy over Jesus was temporarily put to rest.

THE ILLUMINATION OF THE TEMPLE

Another ceremony of the feast of Tabernacles, the illumination of the Temple, also had its source in Jewish tradition.

According to the Mishna, at the end of the first day of Tabernacles, the priests and Levites went down to the court of the women. Four enormous golden candlesticks were set up in the court (fifty cubits high) with four golden bowls placed upon them and four ladders resting against each. Four youths of priestly descent stood at the top of the ladders holding ten-gallon pitchers filled with pure oil, which they poured into each bowl (Sukkah 5:2).

The priests and Levites used their own worn-out liturgical clothing for wicks. The light emanating from the four candelabra was so bright that the Mishna says, "There was no courtyard in Jerusalem that was not lit up with the light at the libation water-well ceremony" (Sukkah 5:3).

The mood was festive. Pious men, members of the Sanhedrin, and heads of the different religious schools would dance well into the night holding burning torches and singing songs of praise to God. The Levitical musicians played spirited music with harps, lyres, cymbals, trumpets,

and, as the Mishna says, "with other instruments of music
without number" (Sukkah 5:4). The Levitical musicians
stood upon the fifteen steps leading down from the court of
the Israelites to the women's court, which, according to
the Mishna, corresponded with the fifteen songs of ascent
in the psalms (Psalms 120-134). Not only did they play instruments with fervor, but the Levitical choir stood chanting and singing as the leaders of Israel danced. Jerusalem
glistened like a diamond that night, and her light could be
seen from afar.

The festivities continued long into the night. Two
priests stood at the Upper Gate (Nicanor Gate), which led
down from the Israelites' court to the court of the women,
and held trumpets in their hands. They waited for the signal—a cock's crow at dawn. Then they sounded a prolonged blast, a quavering note, and another prolonged blast
of the shofar. They then held their trumpets without sound
and proceeded to the tenth step, where they sounded another prolonged blast, a quavering note, and a prolonged
blast. Finally, when they reached the court of the women
they blew another prolonged blast, quavering note, and
prolonged blast. The momentum intensified, and the two
priests began blowing prolonged blasts until they reached
the gate that led to the east (the Beautiful Gate). Once
through the gate with a multitude of worshipers, they
turned their faces towards the west, facing the sanctuary in
the Temple. With the sun rising and the light of the candelabra paling, they chanted an ancient prayer: "Our ancestors, when they were in this place, turned with their backs
unto the Temple and their faces towards the east and they
prostrated themselves eastward toward the sun, but as for
us our eyes are turned to the eternal." It was a magnificent
ceremony filled with beauty and symbolism. The light represented the Shekinah glory that once filled the Temple.[5]

5. Edersheim, p. 285.

But the brightness of the holy city at the ceremony of illumination paled in the presence of Jesus. In the brilliance of the gloriously lit Temple Jesus cried, "I am the light of the world; he who follows Me shall not walk in the darkness, but shall have the light of life" (John 8:12). He was more glorious than Herod's Temple, for He embodied the Shekinah, and in Him dwelt the fullness of God (Colossians 1:19). Once the pilgrims had seen Him, they had seen the Father; for in Jesus, God had stepped outside the Holy of Holies to dwell with men.

This pronouncement of Jesus caused another controversy with the Pharisees, who argued that Jesus was simply bearing witness of Himself and therefore His witness was false. But ultimately Jesus said, "The Father who sent Me bears witness of Me" (John 8:18).

There is some question as to when exactly the encounter with the adulterous woman in 8:1-11 took place. Evangelical scholars disagree as to whether or not John 8:1-11 is part of the original autographs. And those who view it as original believe that its placement in the gospel of John was arbitrary.[6] Either way, if this incident is removed it would allow the two statements to be seen in sequence. For indeed it does seem logical that the statement of Jesus beginning in 8:12 should follow chronologically after His declaration in 7:38.

Regardless, the truth of Jesus' statement is dramatically proved in the next chapter, where He is seen healing the man born blind (John 9). It is interesting to note the allusions to the two ceremonies of Tabernacles. Jesus said, "While I am in the world, I am the light of the world" (John 9:5), a possible reference to the ceremony of the illumination of the Temple. After this, He spat on the ground and made clay, applying it to the eyes of the blind man and say-

6. A. T. Robertson, *A Harmony of the Gospels* (New York: Harper & Row, 1950), p. 115; Tenney, p. 89.

ing, "Go, wash in the pool of Siloam" (John 9:7). When the blind man obeyed, he was healed. At the ceremony of the water drawing, the people's attention was focused on this pool. The two remarkable claims Jesus made at the feast of Tabernacles were verified in the healing of the man born blind.

In Jesus the Messiah we see the fulfillment of the feast of Tabernacles. John wrote: "And the Word became flesh, and dwelt among us, and we beheld His glory, glory as of the only begotten from the Father, full of grace and truth" (John 1:14).

Jesus is God tabernacling among men. The word *dwelt* in Greek implies a temporary dwelling, a sukkah booth. Jesus is God's ultimate sukkah booth. For God, in Jesus Christ, tabernacled among men. As the Temple was a temporary dwelling for the Shekinah, so Jesus tabernacling among us manifested the glory of God. He is the source of light and life to all who believe.

16

Jewish Observance of Sukkot

PREPARATION FOR SUKKOT

As the sun sets signaling the end of Yom Kippur, the Jewish family drives the first nail of the sukkah booth. The teachers of Israel say that it is a duty to begin building the booth after the Day of Atonement. Even if it is a Sabbath eve, the booth is still to be started, because one should not delay the fulfilling of a commandment when he has the opportunity to do so immediately. Such is the expectation, the anticipated joyful relief that is attached to the final feast of Tishri.

BUILDING THE BOOTH

The building of the booth is one of the most exciting parts of the celebration of Sukkot, especially for the children. Older youths are assigned the heavy labor of gathering the materials and sawing, nailing, and constructing the frame of the booth, while the adults supervise. They need to ensure that the booth will be high enough for a tall man to comfortably stand and wide enough for the family table with room for guests to sit in comfort. The sukkah is built outdoors, in the yard or possibly even on the roof if no yard space is available—but never under a tree, for that would be in violation of rabbinic laws. The family may never know the reason, but it is tradition.

It is likely that the sukkah will have only three walls, one of which may be a wall of the house. Instead of a door, a curtain or drape hangs over the fourth side.

After the walls are finished, the roof is erected. Here is where the youths need to be careful, for the rabbis have specific rules telling how a sukkah roof is to be built. The proper building materials are essential. Palm branches are ideal, but, whatever foliage is used, the family is careful that it is something that grew out of the earth and could not have been defiled according to Levitical laws. The branches have to be placed with great care, as the roof has to be open enough for the inhabitants to see the stars at night and allow some rain to penetrate, but not so open that it lets in more sunshine than shadow during the day. This requires the skill of an experienced sukkah "maven" (or expert) but is no problem, for most youths watch in fascination from their childhood as their older relatives, year in and year out, carefully climb ladders and construct the sukkah roofs.

BEAUTIFYING THE BOOTH

Once the sukkah itself is erected, it is time for the smaller children to join the project. They are excited to do their part in fulfilling the tradition of beautifying the sukkah. For if there is one thing the Jewish people agree on regarding the festival of Sukkot, it is that the mere building of the sukkah booth is never considered enough. The sukkah must be made as beautiful as it can be. The rabbis say that the verse "This is my God, and I will praise Him" (Exodus 15:2) is really speaking about the booths of Sukkot, and therefore it is a duty to "make a beautiful sukkah in His honor" (Shabbat 133b).

This glad duty is not left without rabbinic advice—the Talmud contains many discussions on how to beautify the festival booths, and Jewish communities around the world have developed their own embellishments as well. For instance, it is customary in many nations to suspend from the roof the seven species of the land of Israel mentioned in Deuteronomy 8:8—wheat, barley, vines, figs, pomegranates, olives, and honey—in gratitude for the Lord's bounty.

As time has passed, the festival ornaments have expanded to include tapestries and bright tablecloths to cover the walls and expensive rugs for the floors. Different cultures use items as diverse as eggs, stuffed birds, paper flowers and chains, and ornamental lanterns to further beautify the booths. In fact, an entire folk art of sukkah decoration has developed over the centuries.

SUKKOT HOSPITALITY

One of the popular ornaments found in the sukkah is a decorated plaque bearing the *Ushpizin*, the fascinating prayer of invitation to "holy guests," which is recited as one enters the sukkah. According to one tradition, the sukkah commemorates the booth built by Abraham when he greeted the three angels (Numbers Rabbah 14): "The Children of Israel were divinely protected in the wilderness by the shelter of the tabernacles solely because the Patriarch Abraham had given shelter to three strangers beneath the tree on his property" (Genesis Rabbah 48:10).

This remembrance of Abraham highlights his outstanding trait of hospitality. The Zohar, a compilation of Jewish mystical writings, embellished this with the tradition of Ushpizin, or "heavenly guests," who visit the booth each night of Sukkot. Abraham, of course, is the first guest. Then, on subsequent nights, come Isaac, Jacob, Moses, Aaron, Joseph, and King David.

The concept of an open door to "holy guests" and to the poor and needy is an integral part of the sukkah, for no "holy guests" would deign to enter a booth where the poor were not welcome.

One modern alternative to inviting needy people to the sukkah is bringing the sukkah to *them*! Unique to our generation is the "sukkahmobile," sponsored by a group of ultra-orthodox Jews. Since the Talmud allows the building of a sukkah on a wagon (Sukkah 2:3), it is not surprising to hear of a portable sukkah that stops at schools, hospitals, shopping centers, and other public institutions. Passersby are invited to enter the "sukkahmobile" and fulfill their duty by pronouncing the proper benedictions.

Back at the family sukkah, the children, armed with their autumn fruits, vegetables, and gourds, are set loose to hang their delicious ornaments on the booth. The decorations are not to be treated lightly—once they are hung they play a role in the performance of the commandment and cannot be used until the end of the holiday:

> If one covered the sukkah to meet its requirements, and adorned it with embroidered hangings and sheets, and hung therein nuts, almonds, peaches, pomegranates, clusters of grapes, wreaths of ears of corn, [phials of] wine, oil or fine flour, it is forbidden to make use of them [for instance, to eat any of the fruit] until the conclusion of the last day of the festival. (Sukkah 10a-b)

THE LULAV AND ETROG

Before the celebration can begin, the father must obtain a proper lulav and etrog. What exactly *are* these mysterious symbols? Jewish tradition traces their origins to the Scriptures: "You shall take for yourselves the foliage of beautiful trees, palm branches and boughs of leafy trees and willows of the brook; and you shall rejoice before the Lord your God for seven days" (Leviticus 23:40).

Long ago there arose a controversy as to whether this passage referred to the actual building of the booths or to a separate commandment to rejoice before the Lord with specific branches and leaves.

The actual terms *lulav* and *etrog* are not found in the Bible but rather began to be used in the time of the Talmudic rabbis. The word *lulav*, which originally meant "a sprout," came to refer to the willow, myrtle, and palm branches that are bound together and waved in rejoicing during the festival of Sukkot.

Etrog, an Aramaic word meaning "that which shines," speaks of a citrus fruit, the citron, which is carried along with the lulav. The citron is a fragrant golden oval or oblong fruit, somewhat larger than a lemon, with a small stem at the base and a slightly knobby projection at the head.

Since there is no mention of the etrog in the Bible, why do the rabbis say that it is the fruit that properly fulfills the commandment? The rabbis tell us that the biblical phrase "the [fruit] of goodly trees" (KJV) implied that *both* tree and fruit had to be goodly, which meant that the taste of the wood and the fruit must be similar. Only the etrog fulfilled both of these requirements. In fact, some rabbis even claim that the tree of knowledge of good and evil in the Garden of Eden was the etrog tree, since the Scriptures say in Genesis 3:6—"the woman saw that the tree was good for eating." What other tree was there whose wood and fruit were both edible? Only the etrog! To further settle the issue, "Eleazar of Worms, a rabbi with a mathematical flair, scientifically and conclusively proved that the fruit of the commandment was the etrog by showing that the numerical value of the Hebrew letters spelling out 'fruit of a goodly tree' was the same as of those in the word 'etrogim.' "[1]

However, the word *hadar* used in the passage and translated "beautiful," or "goodly," is associated with the idea of beauty, adornment, or splendor. Some Jewish commentators believe the root of the word to be "dur," meaning that which remains on the tree from year to year (Sukkah 35a).

---

1. Goodman, p. 158.

It can then be taken to mean any kind of citrus fruit: lemon, lime, orange, and so on.

Rabbinic tradition gives considerable attention to the requirements regarding the four species of plants mentioned in Leviticus:

"The fruit of goodly trees" refers to the etrog, or citron, which must be beautiful and fragrant, with no blemish or deficiency found in it.

"Branches of palm trees" are the actual lulav, or palm branch, beautiful but scentless. The lulav must be at least three handbreaths high and fit to be shaken. Each branch must be taken fresh, entire, unpolluted, and not from an idolatrous grove.

"Boughs of leafy trees" are three myrtle twigs, humble but sweet-smelling, and containing more leaves than berries.

"Willows of the brook" are two simple willow leaves, the kind that grow in abundance along bodies of water.

There are numerous explanations of the meaning of the four species themselves. One is that each of the four items refers to a particular limb through which man is to serve God:

> The Etrog refers to the heart—the place of understanding and wisdom.
> The Lulav refers to the backbone—uprightness.
> The Myrtle corresponds to the eyes—enlightenment.
> The Willow represents the lips—the service of the lips (prayer).[2]

Some rabbis say that the four species are intended to remind Israel of the different stages of their wilderness journey, as represented by the different vegetation:

2. Siegel and Strassfeld, p. 75.

The palm branches recall the valleys and plains.
The "boughs of thick trees," the bushes on the mountain heights.
The "willows" those brooks from which God had given His people to drink.
The etrog was to remind people of the fruits of the good land which the Lord had given them.[3]

Another explanation is that the four species symbolize the characters and virtues of the ancient patriarchs. The number of interpretations is endless, but one is quoted below which bears careful reading:

"The product of goodly trees" [the etrog] standing for [some men in] Israel: even as the etrog has aroma and has edible fruit, so Israel have in their midst men who have knowledge of Torah and also have good deeds.
"Branches of palm trees" also stands for [some men in] Israel: as the palm tree has edible fruit but no aroma, so Israel have in their midst men who have knowledge of Torah but have not good deeds.
"Boughs of leafy trees" also stands for [some men in] Israel: as the myrtle tree has aroma but has not edible fruit, so Israel have in their midst men who have good deeds but have not Torah.
"And willows of the brook" also stands for [some men in] Israel: even as the willow has neither edible fruit nor aroma, so Israel have in their midst men in whom there is neither knowledge of Torah nor good deeds.
The Holy One says. In order to make it impossible for Israel to be destroyed, let all of them be bound together as plants are bound into a cluster, so that the righteous among them will atone for the others. Hence Moses charged Israel: "Take for your own sake on the first day [a cluster] [Leviticus 23:40]." (Pesikta Rabbati 51:2)

3. Edersheim, p. 275.

THE WAVING OF THE LULAV

Technically, the lulav itself is the single palm branch that occupies the central position in the arrangement. It has a holderlike bottom (made from its own leaves), with the two willow branches to its left and the three myrtle branches to its right. This cluster is held in the right hand, and the etrog, or citron, is held in the left. These are taken and waved in the synagogue on the morning of each of the seven days of Sukkot (except on the Sabbath). This waving takes place at specific points in the liturgy, while a blessing is said: "Blessed art Thou, O Lord our God, King of the Universe, who hast sanctified us with Thy commandments and has commanded us concerning the waving of the lulav."

To wave the lulav properly, one must stand facing east, shake the cluster slowly and deliberately three times, and repeat the motion to the south, to the west, to the north, above one's head, and down towards the floor. Tradition gives the following meaning of this elaborate ritual: "The four directions of the compass remind us of God, to whom the four directions belong, and the lulav is waved up and down in acknowledgment of Him to whom are heaven and earth" (Sukkah 37b).

These wavings serve to arouse joy, thanksgiving, and praise of God at the time of the final fruit harvest.

Every man must have his own lulav. One cannot borrow a lulav to use but may receive it as a gift, even if that gift was given on the condition that it be returned.

So with lulav and etrog firmly in hand, the family goes to the synagogue. After the service, cake, fruit, wine, and other refreshments are provided in the congregational sukkah. But nobody eats much on this night, for each participant can almost taste the feast that lies ahead in his own sukkah booth. After the refreshments, the family rushes home for their own celebration.

THE EVENING IN THE SUKKAH

When they return to the sukkah, they are proud of their creation. There, on the floor, lies a colorful rug. Clusters of grapes, apples, gourds, and vegetables hang on strings from the thatched roof. Cranberries are strung from one corner to another. The children's own drawings are proudly displayed on the wooden walls. The structure is no longer merely a leafy booth—it is a work of art!

THE BLESSINGS

But the gaiety is suspended for a moment as they enter the sukkah, and the father recites the traditional blessing: "Blessed art Thou, O Lord our God, King of the universe, who has sanctified us with Thy commandments and commanded us to dwell in a booth."

He then continues with this meditation:

> I have gone forth from my home to this tabernacle because I would walk firmly in the way of Thy commandments wherever they may take me.
>
> Lord, pour out on me Thy great blessings and give me life, and when the time must come that I shall leave this world, may mine be the merit of dwelling in the cover of Thy protecting wings. Yet may it be my lot to be sealed in the Book of Life on earth for many days to come, and living in the Holy Land in reverent service of Thee. Blessed evermore be the Lord. Amen.[4]

Once they have entered the booth, the family members take a few moments to reflect on the nature of this sukkah booth that will become their home and shelter for the remainder of the holiday. The father reminds his children that

4. David de Sola Pool, ed. and trans., *The Traditional Prayer Book for Sabbath and Festivals* (New York: Behrman House, 1960), p. 636.

a man must not put his trust in the size or strength or salutary conveniences of his house, even though it be filled with the best of everything; nor should he rely upon the help of any man, even though he be the lord of the land. But let him put his trust in Him Whose word called the universe into being, for He alone is mighty and faithful, and He does not retract what He promises.[5]

The sukkah reminds us of the humility that we must have before God:

Do not say in your heart, "My own power and the might of my own hand have won this wealth for me" (Deuteronomy 8:17); you should remember the Lord your God, as it is He who gives you strength to make progress. Therefore, the people leave [their] houses, which are full of everything good at the season of ingathering, and dwell in booths, as a reminder of those who had no possessions in the wilderness and no houses in which to live. For this reason, the Holy One established the feast of Tabernacles at the time of the ingathering from the threshing floor and the wine press, that the people should not be proud of their well-furnished houses.[6]

THE MEAL

After these and more meditations are recited, the time arrives for the family meal. In the glow of the holiday candles, shadows dance on the dimly lit walls. The blessings over the foods are chanted, and then, in the fresh open air, delicious aromas from the kitchen begin to combine with the pungent smell of the foliage and decorations. The time for the meal has come!

Jewish people must sleep, eat, drink, and live in the Sukkah exactly as they live in their houses the rest of the

5. Isaac Aboab, in *Menorat ha-Maor* 3.6.1. Cited in Goodman, p. 53.
6. Rashbam (Samuel ben Meir), Leviticus 23:43.

year. So of course, the finest of linens, dishes, and silver-
ware are used when living in the booth.

There is no Jewish food that is universally eaten on
Sukkot. Each culture has different customs—Yemenite
Jews slaughter a sheep or an ox to eat for the entire festival; in Germany, stuffed cabbage is eaten on the last day of
the feast; Eastern European Jews traditionally serve *kreplach* (pieces of dough filled with chopped meat) during
Tabernacles. Special holiday cakes, strudels, and festive
candies are popular as well.

On the feast of Booths, even ordinary bread becomes
transformed, since it is often baked in symbolic shapes,
such as a ladder for the ascent of prayers to heaven, a key
for the opening of the heavenly portals, or a hand for receiving the divine decree for the New Year. And as on Rosh
Hashanah, bread is dipped in honey to symbolize the festival's joyfulness.

SLEEPING IN THE SUKKAH

After the meal is over and the holiday songs have been
sung, the family retires to sleep in the sukkah for the night.
That is, of course, unless it rains; for if the sukkah was
properly constructed the celebrants would get quite wet.

What does one do if it rains? Some rabbis say that
nothing must be done to lessen the discomfort of dwelling
in booths—even rain can be bailed out only if it "threatens
to spoil the gruel." Others, however, tell us that the laws of
dwelling in booths don't apply in case of severe discomfort
(Sukkah 2:9). If rain has continued for more than two
hours, one may recite the blessing, eat a small piece of
bread (about the size of an olive) in the booth, and proceed
to the house for the rest of the meal. Even in a light rain,
one may sleep inside his house instead (Kitzur Shulhan

Arukh 134-35). And if one is ill, of course, he is exempt
from the commandment (Sukkah 26a).

For the next seven days and nights, the religious family will live in the sukkah. A favorite pastime of Sukkot is
visiting the neighbors' booths and admiring each others'
decorations—each person, or course, being sure that none
surpasses his own in beauty and creativity.

Hoshana Rabbah

The holiday continues much in the same manner day
after day until the last day of the feast. The seventh and
last day of Sukkot, known as Hoshana Rabbah, "The Great
Hosanna," is somewhat a festival in itself. On other days of
the feast, when the family goes to synagogue, one procession is made around the sanctuary with lulav and etrog
while the congregation sings, "*Hosheanah*, save us." This
particular tradition is believed to date back to the time of
the Maccabees, around 165 B.C.

On the final day, the entire congregation marches
around *seven times*, carrying even more willow leaves with
them. These seven times, a memorial of the circuits made
by the ancient priests around the Temple altar during worship, remind us of God's goodness in destroying Jericho
once Israel had circled it seven times.

After the seventh time around the synagogue, the willow branches are beaten until their leaves fall off—a symbol of beating off our sins and a prayer for plenteous water
for next year's willows. Many religious Jews save these willow branches and use them to kindle the fire in which the
first unleavened bread for Passover is baked half a year
later.

In contrast to the festive days of Sukkot, Hoshana
Rabbah is observed solemnly, as an extension of the Day of
Atonement. On this day, the rabbis tell us, the gates of
judgment finally close and the decrees pronounced by God

on the Day of Atonement take effect. In fact, it is customary for religious Jews to stay awake the entire night before Hoshana Rabbah, studying the Bible and praying the traditional prayers for rain for the coming year.

SHEMINI ATZERET

The last day of the festival of Sukkot is called Shemini Atzeret, both in the Bible and in rabbinic literature. Shemini Atzeret, the Eighth Day of Solemn Assembly, was treated by Talmudic rabbis as a separate festival. This has changed, and today it is mostly regarded as the conclusion of the feast of Tabernacles and the beginning of the next agricultural year.

The Talmud explains the nature of the holiday in the following parable:

> A king once gave a feast to which the diplomatic representatives of many nations were invited. The feast lasted for seven days. When they were all ready to depart, the king called aside his son who was also among the guests and said to him, "While all these strangers were around we hardly had an opportunity to have an intimate conversation. Tarry thou one day longer, when we shall hold a simple feast all by ourselves." Thus, God arranged for the feast of Sukkot when seventy offerings are made in behalf of the seventy nations of the world. On the conclusion of the feast, He begs of Israel to tarry [atzar, "hold, keep back"] one day longer when only one bullock and one ram are offered in behalf of Israel.[7]

Israel, acting in intercession for the world on the seven days of Sukkot, takes this one last day to be alone with God.

Today, Jewish families will still eat in the festival booth on Shemini Atzeret. The liturgy for this day contains

7. Goodman, pp. 134-35.

a memorial service and a special prayer for rain for the coming season. Often, the children's teachers are called upon to say this prayer, since their high calling gives them a better chance to be answered by God.

The book of Ecclesiastes is read on Shemini Atzeret. It is melancholy in nature and appropriate for this autumn festival. The reading of Ecclesiastes, with its emphasis on vanity, serves to temper excessive exultation on this holiday.[8]

SIMCHAT TORAH

Simchat Torah is a separate holiday that falls on the day after Sukkot, the same day as Shemini Atzeret, although outside of Israel it is celebrated for two days. This holiday is mentioned neither in the Scriptures nor in the Talmud. It is likely that it dates back to the post-Talmudic period, but we do not find it being observed until the eleventh century in Western Europe.[9]

The joyfulness of Sukkot is dim compared to the exuberance displayed during the Simchat Torah celebrations, for Simchat Torah means "rejoicing in the law." This festival is one of the most energetic of the Jewish year.

The festival of Simchat Torah commemorates the closing of the annual Torah-reading cycle and the beginning of a new one. Each week in the synagogue, a portion of the five books of Moses is read in a specified order, so that the entire five books are covered during a one-year cycle. Actually, an older tradition that is still practiced by some Jewish cultures is to complete the cycle of Torah-reading in three years instead of one, but among Western Jews the yearly cycle has prevailed. The rabbis say that Israel's adherence to a Torah-reading cycle is a symbol of their

8. Ibid., p. 331.
9. Gaster, p. 99.

loyalty to the Torah and their unconquerable spirit as a people. It is their answer to the command God gave to Joshua: "The Book of the Law shall not depart out of thy mouth, but thou shalt meditate therein day and night, that thou mayest observe to do according to all that is written therein."[10]

Joy in the festival is a religious duty, but not a difficult one to perform. The principle of joy in relation to fulfilling the law has been little understood and is not often mentioned in theological writings. But in Talmudic and devotional Jewish literature of the Middle Ages, a recurring theme is: "Tremble with joy when thou art about to fulfill a commandment."[11]

THE EVENING CELEBRATION

On the evening of Simchat Torah, all the Scrolls of the Law except one are paraded around the synagogue seven times, as the children lead the procession singing, waving flags or carrying apples and candles on tall sticks. The congregation sings and dances, both with the Torah and with each other. In fact, some believe it is meritorious to get a little drunk this evening, since drinking improves one's ability to dance and celebrate, but that is not an approved rabbinic practice.

After they have circled the synagogue seven times, they read the last passage in the book of Deuteronomy, and the books are put back in their place for the night. This is the only time the Torah is read in the synagogue at night.

THE NEXT MORNING

The next morning, the family returns to the synagogue where once more the happy parade begins. Seven times,

10. Goodman, p. 118.
11. Ibid., p. 119.

they circle the sanctuary. Then the last portion of Deuteronomy is read again, closing the yearly cycle, but this time it is followed by the first portion of the book of Genesis. Those chosen to recite these two sections are called "bridegrooms"—the Bridegroom of the Law and the Bridegroom of the First Portion. It is considered an honor to be chosen as one of the bridegrooms on Simchat Torah. These are often the most esteemed men in the community, who pledge contributions to charity and have the privilege of inviting their friends to a great feast after the service (Kitzur Shulhan Arukh 138).

Actually, some believe that the entire celebration prescribed for Simchat Torah closely parallels the Jewish wedding service and in fact symbolizes the marriage of Israel to the law. The bridegrooms, for instance, are attended by "bridesmen." The procession around the synagogue resembles the wedding custom of walking seven times around the bride and groom. In some traditions, fruits and nuts are tossed at the bridegrooms while they read, much as they would be at a wedding. It certainly is a fascinating comparison.

Besides the march around the synagogue with flags and apples, besides the fun and merriment of Simchat Torah, there is still one more coveted privilege given to the children on this day. In the synagogue, all the children under thirteen are called up to say the blessings over the reading of the Torah. It is the only time when such youngsters are allowed to do this, and a rare privilege it is. The little ones are covered with large prayer shawls as they recite the prayers together, and then are blessed by the rabbi with Jacob's words to Ephraim and Manasseh, "The angel who has redeemed me from all evil, bless the lads" (Genesis 48:16).

DISMANTLING THE BOOTH

At the conclusion of Simchat Torah, the family once more sets to work on their booth—this time to dismantle it and perhaps save some portions to use in the following year. But the sad occasion does have its bright point: now the tempting fruits and vegetables can finally be enjoyed, and the family can return to the comfort and warmth of their home. They return, that is, until next year, when this happy holiday beckons them once again to recall God's provision for them in the wilderness so long ago.

17
Tabernacles Tomorrow

The ancient prophets speak about Israel's distant future in great detail: there are prophecies that predict her repentance, redemption, and rejoicing in the coming of her messianic King. But the feasts of the Hebrew calendar are not mentioned—none, that is, except the Passover and Tabernacles (Ezekiel 45:21-25). The prophet Zecharaiah also writes of the celebration of Sukkot in the future. The Lord deems this feast so important that the Gentiles are commanded to observe it as well. The prophet states: "Then it will come about that any who are left of all the nations that went against Jerusalem will go up from year to year to worship the King, the Lord of hosts, and to celebrate the Feast of Booths" (Zechariah 14:16).

The prophet Zechariah wrote of a future day when all the nations of the earth, not only the Jewish people, will be called upon to celebrate the feast of Tabernacles. This command might seem mysterious at first glance, but when viewed in light of Israel's calling and mission, the place accorded Tabernacles is appropriate.

THE CALLING AND MISSION OF ISRAEL

The future observance of Sukkot by the nations of the world rests upon Israel's election and mission. The universal concern of God's plan for the Jewish people reaches back to His covenant with Abraham. In that agreement,

God promised, "And I will bless those who bless you, and the one who curses you I will curse. And in you *all the families of the earth shall be blessed*" (Genesis 12:3, italics added). From Abraham's loins, God would raise up a people, Israel, to be a blessing to the nations. Israel's election must always be linked with her mission to the Gentiles. Israel was chosen to be God's vehicle of blessing to the world.

Moses wrote regarding the choosing of Israel:

> For you are a holy people to the Lord your God; the Lord your God has chosen you to be a people for His own possession out of all the peoples who are on the face of the earth. The Lord did not set His love on you nor choose you because you were more in number than any of the peoples, for you were the fewest of all peoples. (Deuteronomy 7:6-7)

God's choice of Israel was not based upon Abraham's merit or their own. God chose Israel because He *decided* to love that nation. "The Lord loved you and kept the oath which He swore to your forefathers, the Lord brought you out by a mighty hand, and redeemed you from the house of slavery, from the hand of Pharaoh king of Egypt" (Deuteronomy 7:8).

God's love was an electing love. He chose one people as His means to bless all mankind. For some sovereign reason unknown to us, God chose to love the Jewish people and through this nation to express His love for the world.

God's loving choice of Israel does not effect the salvation of individual Jewish people. Rather, God chose a people for *service*—service that was directed toward the rest of the world. So although God limited His line of promise by choosing one nation above the others, His redemptive plan was intended for the entire world.

WITNESSES OF THE ONE TRUE GOD

The prophet Isaiah wrote that the role of the nation of Israel was to be a witness for God: " 'You are My witnesses,' declares the Lord, 'and My servant whom I have chosen, in order that you may know and believe Me, and understand that I am He. Before Me there was no God formed, and there will be none after Me' " (Isaiah 43:10; cf. 43:12; 44:8).

In this verse, the prophet set the scene of a cosmic law court, where God is the judge and the nations of the world stand trial for their idolatry. Israel is the star witness for the prosecution. They were chosen to hold aloft a testimony of the uniqueness of their God. The Lord, speaking through Isaiah, says, "I, even I, am the Lord; and there is no savior besides Me" (Isaiah 43:11). What was Israel's mission? To proclaim to the world that the God of Israel is the only true God and there is no other Savior but He.

MISSIONARY PRIESTS

Israel was to be more than a witness to the nations; they were also to be an intercessor on the nations' behalf. They were commissioned for this holy responsibility at Mount Sinai. God said to Moses,

> You yourselves have seen what I did to the Egyptians, and how I bore you on eagles' wings, and brought you to Myself. Now then, if you will indeed obey My voice and keep My covenant, then you shall be My own possession among all the peoples, for all the earth is Mine; and you shall be to Me a kingdom of priests and a holy nation. (Exodus 19:4-6)

Once again God expressed His concern for the world when He declared, "All the earth is Mine." He chose Israel from among all the peoples of the earth for an eternal pur-

pose—that they might be His vehicle to restore and reclaim a rebellious world. Israel was not chosen for their
own sake, but for the sake of the nations. God describes
their unique position as "a kingdom of priests." Their role
was to intercede with a holy God for a sinful world.

In the passage above, God called the people by an en-
dearing term, *segullah,* translated "possession," but perhaps better translated as "special treasure." Although
Israel was to be God's treasure and possession, they must
never forget that the entire world belonged to the Lord and
was the subject of His concern.

ISRAEL'S FAILURE

Israel failed in their mission to reach the world. Not
only were they disobedient to the commandments of God,
but they did not extend themselves in missionary activity.
And yet, the God of all grace did not renege on His choice.
He would still use the nation of Israel to bless the world.

Israel did not fulfill their mission, but God completed
the task Himself. He sent His Son Jesus to live perfectly under the law, to be a light to the nations and to intercede
once for all on behalf of Jews and Gentiles. The faithlessness of man can never thwart the faithfulness of God. The
Gentiles most assuredly would share in the salvation
brought by the Divine Seed of Abraham. Paul wrote:

> Christ redeemed us from the curse of the Law, having
> become a curse for us—for it is written, "Cursed is ev-
> eryone who hangs on a tree"—in order that in Christ Je-
> sus the blessing of Abraham might come to the Gentiles,
> so that we might receive the promise of the Spirit
> through faith. (Galatians 3:13-14)

It is tempting for some to think that Israel's role in
world redemption is finished. But that is not true. For although Israel failed in their mission, they remain chosen

(Romans 11:25-29) and still have a role to play in the future. The apostle Paul declared: "Now if their transgression be riches for the world and their failure be riches for the Gentiles, how much more will their fulfillment be!" (Romans 11:12). And again he wrote, "For if their rejection be the reconciliation of the world, what will their acceptance be but life from the dead?" (Romans 11:15).

The apostle spoke of a future time when Israel will once again don the mantle of obligation and fulfill their role as a missionary nation. In some remarkable way the nation of Israel will again be used by God to bring the message of the Messiah to the nations; for Israel will be central to His kingdom ministry.

Isaiah spoke of a day when Jerusalem would be restored, both physically and spiritually:

> For Zion's sake I will not keep silent, and for Jerusalem's sake I will not keep quiet, until her righteousness goes forth like brightness, and her salvation like a torch that is burning. And the nations will see your righteousness, and all kings your glory; and you will be called by a new name, which the mouth of the Lord will designate. You will also be a crown of beauty in the hand of the Lord, and a royal diadem in the hand of your God. (Isaiah 62:1-3)

In that day, Israel will not be the tail, but the head of the nations (Deuteronomy 28:13). Jerusalem will be the spiritual focal point of the world because the King of Jerusalem, the Prince of Peace, will reign in His chosen city. Isaiah wrote of that joyful occasion: "Break forth, shout joyfully together, you waste places of Jerusalem; for the Lord has comforted His people, He has redeemed Jerusalem. The Lord has bared His holy arm in the sight of all the nations, that all the ends of the earth may see the salvation of our God" (Isaiah 52:9-10).

The day is coming when a restored and renewed Israel will once again become a light to the nations, for the destiny of Israel is linked to the destiny of the world. Their testimony will be glorious and true because the One who is all-glorious in truth will sit upon His throne. In that day, the Jewish people will be "life from the dead" for the nations of the earth.

UNIVERSAL THEMES IN THE FEAST OF TABERNACLES

God's concern for the Gentiles is most evident in the Talmudic writings regarding Sukkot. In Jewish sources, Israel's role in world redemption is a major theme of the feast of Tabernacles. This is reiterated in the midrash on Psalm 109:4: "At the festival of Tabernacles we offer up seventy bullocks (as an atonement) for the seventy nations, and we pray that rain will come down for them."[1]

Israel is considered a nation of intercessors for the sins of the Gentiles. That universal theme is also recounted in the later and more mystical literature of the Kaballah and the Zohar.

ZECHARIAH 14

The traditional Bible reading on the second day of Sukkot is taken from the fourteenth chapter of the book of Zechariah. An additional portion read on Sukkot speaks about the war of Gog and Magog (Ezekiel 38:14–39:16). This seems incongruous—what thematic relationship does this Scripture portion have to the feast of Booths? Although it may not be evident to the casual reader, the common thread uniting these two passages is God's universal concern for the redemption of the nations. In Zechariah 14, the judgment against rebellious nations will be that God withholds life-giving rains. The judgment in Ezekiel 38

1. Goodman, p. 43.

upon hostile nations will also be rain—judgment rain of "hailstones, fire, and brimstone" (v. 22). The Lord declared, "I shall magnify Myself, sanctify Myself, and make Myself known in the sight of many nations; and they will know that I am the Lord" (v. 23). Whether in blessing or in judgment, God intends to show the nations that He is the Lord.

THE MEANING OF THE PROPHECY

The prophet Zechariah spoke of the end of days, when Israel and the nations will celebrate the feast of Tabernacles. In that day, Israel will be redeemed and her enemies destroyed.

The day of restoration will take place after the "time of Jacob's distress" (Jeremiah 30:7), or, in the New Testament, the Great Tribulation (Matthew 24:21). The prophet wrote of Israel's indescribable agony during this terrible period:

> "And it will come about in all the land," declares the Lord, "that two parts in it will be cut off and perish; but the third will be left in it. And I will bring the third part through the fire, refine them as silver is refined, and test them as gold is tested. They will call on My name, and I will answer them; I will say, 'They are My people,' and they will say, 'The Lord is my God.'" (Zechariah 13:8-9)

From the midst of this great tribulation, the Jewish people will cry out to God; and in His great mercy, the Lord will send His Messiah, Jesus, to deliver them from destruction (Zechariah 12:10). Israel will be restored, both spiritually and nationally. Her enemies will be crushed, and the Messiah will reign, not over Israel alone but over *all* the nations of the earth: "The Lord will be king over all the earth; in that day the Lord will be the only one, and His name the only one" (Zechariah 14:9).

God's plan for the heathen is not to destroy them but to bring them into subjection at His feet. He will command the faithful among the Gentiles to come to Jerusalem and celebrate the feast of Booths (Zechariah 14:16). Why did God choose Sukkot, and not one of the other major festivals, as the test of obedience for the Gentiles?

Some scholars believe that Sukkot, as the feast of Ingathering, is the most appropriate time for God to gather the human fruit for His kingdom.[2] Others believe that the heathen, who have been brought out of the wanderings of this life into the blessedness of God's kingdom, celebrate the feast of Thanksgiving out of their overflowing gratefulness to the God who redeemed them.[3]

Most important, though, Zechariah describes the conversion of the nations to the one true God. In every age, God gives His people obligations. The feast of Tabernacles must be viewed as one of the kingdom obligations of the Gentiles. It is their opportunity to worship God as well as His test point for their obedience. The prophet warned the recalcitrant and disobedient nations that there would be stinging judgment for any who would not keep the feast. The judgment, in keeping with the theme of the feast of Ingathering, calls for God to withhold rain. If the nations were not willing to worship God in Jerusalem, He would withhold the provision of food as well as His blessings.

We would be remiss not to mention the ultimate and eternal significance of the feast of Tabernacles. The apostle John wrote:

> And I heard a loud voice from the throne, saying, "Behold, the tabernacle of God is among men, and He shall dwell among them, and they shall be His people, and

2. Charles Lee Feinberg, *God Remembers: A Study of the Book of Zechariah* (New York: American Board of Missions to the Jews, 1965), p. 261.
3. Keil and Delitzsch, vol. 6, p. 1499.

God Himself shall be among them, and He shall wipe away every tear from their eyes; and there shall no longer be any death; there shall no longer be any mourning, crying, or pain; the first things have passed away." (Revelation 21:3-4)

Ultimately, the whole earth will become the sukkah booth of God, and He will reign in the presence of His Son for all eternity. This reminds us of Solomon's prayer, where he understood clearly God's intention to fill His redeemed earth with His very presence. Doesn't this give a whole new perspective to why Tabernacles is called the season of our joy? What greater joy can there be than to be in the presence of God forever?

Conclusion:
The Lord of Your Life

Jesus is Lord of the calendar, but is He Lord of your life? That question must be addressed before this book is put to rest. It would be possible to read through the entire volume, grasping the content without understanding the message for the heart. The core of the book is not about festivals but about a relationship. The fall feasts were holy occasions for Israel to celebrate their relationship to God and affirm Him as their Sovereign.

The feasts were given to Israel within the boundaries of their relationship to God. Outside that covenant relationship they become mere religious ceremonies. God does not merely call upon us to fulfill certain religious duties and obligations; He calls us into a relationship in which we renounce our rebellion and commit ourselves to Him as loyal subjects. That is the message of the fall feasts: that we might commit our lives to God and crown the Lord of the universe Lord of our lives.

REPENTANCE

The feast of Rosh Hashanah teaches the first step in discovering a personal relationship with God. The theme of the Day of Trumpets is *repentance*. The haunting notes of the shofar remind us of God's relationship with Abraham. That same relationship, the chance to be a "friend of God," is available to us today. To heed the call of the shofar we must repent, turning away from sin and toward God.

The first step is the most difficult. It requires a great deal of courage for us to confront our unrighteousness. Reciting the great confessions repeated during the festival is not sufficient, as some sin we have committed might escape mention. We must agree with the prophet that "all of our righteous deeds are like a filthy garment" (Isaiah 64:6). Our helplessness will lead us to true repentance. We must approach God admitting that we have nothing to offer but our willingness to serve Him.

Repentance is more than saying, "I'm sorry," or asking for forgiveness. Repentance means being sorry enough to change. It means being willing to make amends to the person we've offended. Good intentions are only part of the process. We must agree to "do righteousness" as well.

Daily repentance is required of all who would follow the Lord. Until the day comes when sin is removed, even the most faithful of us will stumble. But this can occur in any relationship, human or divine. When we wrong someone, we must apologize. A strong relationship, whether between a man and wife or between friends, will survive any number of blows. And so will our walk with God—if we seek His daily cleansing for our sins. The apostle John wrote: "If we confess our sins, He is faithful and righteous to forgive us our sins and to cleanse us from all unrighteousness" (1 John 1:9).

The word *confess* means to agree with God regarding our sin and be willing to change. There is no need to wait for a certain time of the year to repent. For the believer in Messiah, it is a daily duty.

Repentance occurs within a relationship and is motivated by love rather than guilt. Repentance can also be the foundation of a relationship, as when two enemies turn from their quarrels and make peace. God was angry with sinners, but love motivated Him to initiate a truce. He reached out to us through the Messiah. Paul wrote, "But God demonstrates His own love toward us, in that while we were yet sinners, Christ [Messiah] died for us" (Romans 5:8). God has taken the first step towards man, and now it is our turn to respond.

It would be futile and frustrating to begin listing a history of our sins. Certainly we would miss some. Besides, God has a more complete record than we do. We must be willing to turn from an ungodly life towards a life of righteousness. That may sound impossible, but God gives us His Spirit to enable us to please Him. By repenting, we are taking the first step towards a personal relationship with God.

REDEMPTION

Yom Kippur, the Day of Atonement, reminds us that repentance alone cannot bring us into a relationship with God. We have wronged Him, and we must pay the penalty for our sins. But He graciously allowed us to offer a substitutionary sacrifice. The contrite and broken hearts of Old Covenant worshipers had no effect unless the penalty for sin was paid. We can be disgusted with a life of sin and repentant in the depths of our souls, but this does not excuse us from sin's consequences. On the other hand, God's Word says: "The life of the flesh is in the blood, and I have given it to you on the altar to make atonement for your souls; for it is the blood by reason of the life that makes atonement" (Leviticus 17:11).

God sent the Messiah, Jesus, to bear sin's penalty for both Jews and Gentiles. Repentance is not enough! We must also accept His sacrifice as God's merciful provision for our atonement.

Yet just acknowledging that Jesus died in our place is not enough. John wrote, "But as many as received Him to them He gave the right to become children of God, even to those who believe in His name" (John 1:12). The Scriptures ask us to receive Him as our *personal Redeemer*, admitting that it was we who deserved death and not Jesus; it was we who sinned, yet He who suffered.

Jesus not only died for the world, He died for you, and now it is your responsibility to take action. The apostle Paul wrote, "For the wages of sin is death, but the free gift of God is eternal life in Christ Jesus our Lord" (Romans 6:23). It is your choice.

Accept Him as your personal Redeemer—as if you stood by His side moments before the nails were driven into His arms and legs, and gently placed your hands upon His head, by faith transferring your sins to the Son of God.

Accept Him as Lord of your life. Ask the God of the universe to be your Master, that you may serve Him, please Him, and make His kingdom a priority in your life.

Accept Him as your Savior by saying a prayer like this one: "Dear God, I know that I have sinned, and I realize that Jesus is the promised Messiah and Savior from sin. I accept Him now as my personal Redeemer and pray that You will strengthen me by Your Holy Spirit to follow Him for the rest of my days. In the name of the Messiah. Amen."

REJOICING

The cycle of fall feasts is completed with Sukkot, a celebration of joy! The plentiful harvest of crops attests to God's faithfulness to His people as they are faithful to Him. Joy is the fruit of obedience, the reward of having been purged and cleansed through repentance and redemption. The decision to receive Jesus as your Redeemer will bring you joy, for there is no greater joy than knowing you are forgiven. But receiving Jesus is just the beginning of your relationship to God.

Jesus told us how to continue enjoying our relationship to Him when He said, "If you keep My commandments, you will abide in My love; just as I have kept My Father's commandments, and abide in His love. These things I have spoken to you, that My joy may be in you, and that your joy may be made full" (John 15:10-11).

The joy of God comes in a harvest of righteousness. As we obey Him we will know His joy in the depths of our hearts.

The month of Tishri illustrates three remarkable steps leading to a personal relationship with God. The time to pursue this relationship is now. Each step is difficult. Each step takes great personal resolve. As a child ventures forward when he begins to walk, you too must take your first steps towards God. Though scared and stumbling, come to Him, and He will draw near to you. Repent and accept His work of redemption, that you may rejoice forever in Jesus the King.

Glossary

AMIDAH—From a Hebrew word meaning "standing." A portion of the Hebrew synagogue liturgy known as the "Eighteen Benedictions." The prayer is a central part of the liturgy and is recited in a standing position.

ANU AMMEKHA—Hebrew prayer meaning "we are thy people." Recited in the Yom Kippur service.

ATZERET—The eighth day of Succot is known as *Shemlni Atzeret.*

AZAZEL—Name of the goat (scapegoat) driven into the wilderness in the Temple service of Yom Kippur.

BA'AL TEKIAH—A person especially trained to blow the shofar according to Jewish law.

CHERUBIM—The angels who spread their wings over the Holy of Holies and who stood as guardians of the divine Presence.

ETROG—An Aramaic word meaning "that which shines." The citron, a lemonlike fruit, is used on Sukkot as the "fruit of a goodly tree."

GAN EDEN—The Garden of Eden.

GEHENNA—Hebrew word for "hell."

GEHINNOM—Originally an ancient valley, located southwest of Jerusalem, in which people sacrificed children to the god Molech. Used as a synonym of "Gehenna," or "hell."

GEMARA—From the Aramaic word for "completion." The commentary and elaboration of the Mishna text, together known as the Talmud.

GEZER—Site of the discovery of an ancient farmer's calendar, beginning in the fall season.

HADAR—Hebrew word translated "goodly" or "beautiful," interpreted by tradition to refer to the etrog, or citron, used on Sukkot.

HAG—Hebrew word for "feast."

HALLAH—The traditional egg bread eaten on the Sabbath and some festivals.

HANUKKAH—The Jewish feast celebrating the rededication of the Temple following the Maccabean uprising in 168 B.C.

HOSANNA—Hebrew word meaning "save now."

HOSHANA RABBAH—The seventh day of Sukkot, known as the "Great Hosanna."

HOSHEANAH—Hebrew word meaning "save now."

KABALLAH—Jewish mystical writings.

KADDISH—A well-known memorial prayer that does not mention death or dying but rather exalts God.

KADOSH—Hebrew word meaning "holy."

KAFAR—The root of the Hebrew word for "holy."

KAPPAROT—The archaic ritual of slaughtering a fowl on Yom Kippur as a substitutionary sacrifice.

KITTEL—A loose white robe worn by adult males in Orthodox synagogues on Rosh Hashanah and Yom Kippur, as well as on Passover by the leader of the family seder.

KOL NIDRE—The ancient Yom Kippur prayer allowing for cancellation of certain vows.

KOPER—A variation of the Hebrew word for "covering" or "redemption."

KOPHER—Hebrew word meaning "a ransom of money."

KREPLACH—A traditional Jewish dish: three-cornered dough pockets filled with meat or cheese.

LULAV—The willow, myrtle, and palm branches that are bound together and waved in rejoicing during the festival of Sukkot.

MAHZOR—From a Hebrew word meaning "cycle." The mahzor is the prayer book used especially on Rosh Hashanah and Yom Kippur.

MALCHUYOT—The Hebrew word for "sovereignty." One of the three major themes of Rosh Hashanah.

MALKUT—An archaic tradition of symbolic flogging on Yom Kippur as a punishment for one's sins.

MAMRE—The location where God appeared to Abraham, giving the promise of Isaac's birth.

MEGILLAH—The scroll of Esther read on the feast of Purim.

MEKHILTA—From an Aramaic word meaning "a measure." The Mekhilta is a collection of rabbinic legal exegesis on the book of Exodus.

MIKVAH—A public bath used for ritual cleansing.

MISHNA—Literally meaning "repetition," the Mishna is a code of traditional Jewish law, which together with the Gemara composes the Talmud.

MOLECH—The name of the ancient Middle Eastern god to which children were sacrificed by fire.

MUSAF—A portion added to the regular Hebrew liturgy.

NEILAH—Originally the name of the concluding service at the Temple, the Neilah is now the last prayer recited in synagogue on Yom Kippur.

NISSUCH HA MAYIM—The ceremony of the water drawing, which took place during Sukkot in the time of Christ.

SALAHTI—From the word translated "forgiven." A Hebrew prayer recited on Yom Kippur.

SANHEDRIN—A Hebraized form of the Greek word *Synedrion,* meaning "assembly." Around the time of Christ this was the high court of the Jewish people, composed of seventy elders.

SEGULLAH—A Hebrew word meaning "possession" or "special treasure." Used by God when referring to Israel in Exodus 19:4-6.

SELICHOT—Special prayers of repentance and supplication recited the week before Rosh Hashanah.

SHABBAT SHUVAH—The Sabbath that falls in the midst of the Ten Days of Awe, called the "Sabbath of Repentance."

SHAHARIT—The name of the morning synagogue service.

SHEKINAH—Hebrew word meaning "dwelling." Used to refer to the divine Presence.

SHEMINI ATZERET—The eighth day of the feast of Sukkot, a day of solemn assembly sometimes spoken of by the rabbis as a separate festival.

SHETIJAH—Another name for the Foundation Stone that remained in the Holy of Holies after the disappearance of the Ark of the Covenant.

SHEVARIM—Shevarim, or "quavers," are a series of trills, one of the three shofar blasts blown on Rosh Hashanah.

SHOFAROT—Meaning "many shofars." One of the three major themes of Rosh Hashanah.

SH'MA—From Deuteronomy 6:4-7, the cornerstone of the Jewish faith, and the declaration of the Oneness of God.

SIMCHAT TORAH—A holiday, meaning "rejoicing of the law," that falls the day after Sukkot, the same day as Shemini Atzeret. On this day one Torah-reading cycle ends and the next begins.

SUKKAH—Originally meaning "woven," a term for a temporary shelter used on Sukkot, woven together from branches and leaves.

TALMUD—From the Hebrew root *lamad,* meaning "learning" or "instruction," the Talmud is the code of Jewish law that is composed of the Mishna and the Gemara.

TASHLICH—The ceremony of casting one's sins into flowing water on Yom Kippur.

TEKIAH—One of the three prescribed shofar blasts on Rosh Hashanah, the tekiah is a short, abrupt bass note.

TERUAH—A long, resonant blast of the shofar, one of the three prescribed shofar blasts of Rosh Hashanah.

TORAH—The Hebrew name of the Pentateuch, Torah actually refers to both the written and oral codes of Jewish law.

TZIMMES—A traditional Jewish dish: a stew made of carrots or sweet potatoes, prunes, and meat.

UN'SANEH TOKEF—The Hebrew prayer recited as the ark of the Torah is opened on Rosh Hashanah.

URIM AND THUMMIM—A device worn on the high priest's breastplate, used to determine the will of God.

USHPIZIN—A prayer of invitation to "holy guests," displayed as a plaque in the Sukkah.

VIDDUI—A confession of sins recited on Yom Kippur.

YAALEH TAHANUNENU—A Hebrew prayer recited on Yom Kippur, which means, "May our entreaty rise to Thee."

YAVNEH—A city located south of modern Tel Aviv, which became the center of Judaism's reorganization after the fall of the Jerusalem Temple.

YETZER HA-RA—A Hebrew term for the evil inclination in man.

YETZER HA-TOV—A Hebrew term for the good inclination in man.

YIZKOR—A Hebrew prayer, "May God Remember," recited upon the death of loved ones.

YOMA—Aramaic for "The Day," a tractate of the Talmud dealing with the Day of Atonement.

YOM T'RUAH—"Day of Blowing," another name for the Feast of Trumpets in Scripture.

ZEMAN SIMHATENU—"The Season of our Joy," a rabbinic name given to Sukkot.

ZICHRONOT—"Remembrance," one of the three main themes of Rosh Hashanah.

ZOHAR—A compilation of Jewish mystical writings composed in the thirteenth century.

Bibliography

Arzt, Max. *Justice and Mercy: Commentary on the Liturgy of the New Year and the Day of Atonement.* New York: Holt, Rinehart and Winston, 1963.

Belkin, Samuel. *In His Image: The Jewish Philosophy of Man as Expressed in Rabbinic Tradition.* New York: Abelard-Schuman, 1960.

Ben Isaiah, Abraham, and Benjamin Sharfman. *The Pentateuch and Rashi's Commentary.* Brooklyn: S. S. and R. Publishing, 1949.

Blackman, Philip, ed. *Mishnayoth.* Gateshead: Judaica Press, 1977.

Bloch, Abraham P. *The Biblical and Historical Background of the Jewish Holy Days.* New York: KTAV, 1978.

Bokser, Ben Zion, ed. *The High Holyday Prayer Book: Rosh Hashanah and Yom Kippur.* New York: Hebrew Publishing, 1959.

Bruce, F. F. *The Epistle to the Hebrews.* Grand Rapids: Eerdmans, 1964.

Buksbazen, Victor. *The Gospel in the Feasts of Israel.* Fort Washington, Pa.: Christian Literature Crusade, 1954.

Cohen, Abraham. *Everyman's Talmud.* New York: E. P. Dutton, 1949.

De Vaux, Roland. *Ancient Israel: Its Life and Institutions.* Translated by John McHugh. 2d ed. London: Darton, Longman & Todd, 1973.

Edersheim, Alfred. *The Temple: Its Ministry and Services.* Grand Rapids: Eerdmans, 1972.

Encyclopedia Judaica. Jerusalem: Keter Publishing House, 1972.

Feinberg, Charles L. *God Remembers: A Study of the Book of Zechariah.* New York: American Board of Missions to the Jews, 1965.

Form of Prayers for Day of Atonement. Rev. ed. New York: Rosenbaum and Werbelowsky, 1890.

Gaster, Theodore. *Festivals of the Jewish Year.* New York: William Morrow, 1953.

Goldberg, Louis. "Whatever Happened to the Substitute Atonement of the Torah?" In *Issues: A Messianic Jewish Perspective,* 5:7.

Goodman, Phillip. *The Rosh Hashanah Anthology.* Philadelphia: Jewish Publication Society of America, 1973.

————. *The Yom Kippur Anthology.* Philadelphia: Jewish Publication Society of America, 1971.

————. *The Sukkot and Simhat Torah Anthology.* Philadelphia: Jewish Publication Society of America, 1973.

Granzfried, Solomon. *Code of Jewish Law.* Translated by Hyman E. Goldin. New York: Hebrew Publishing, 1949.

Greenstone, Julius H. *Jewish Feasts and Fasts.* Philadelphia: Chautauqua Society, 1945.

A Hebrew and English Lexicon of the Old Testament. Edited by Francis Brown. Translated by Edward Robinson. 1907. Reprint. Oxford: Clarendon Press, 1972.

Hertz, Joseph Herman. *The Authorized Daily Prayer Book.* New York: Bloch Publishing, 1948.

Idelsohn, A. Z. *Jewish Liturgy and Its Development.* New York: Schocken Books, 1972.

Jacobs, Louis. *A Guide to Yom Kippur.* London: Jewish Chronicle Publications, 1957.

————. *A Jewish Theology.* New York: Behrman House, 1973.

Jeremias, Joachim. *Jerusalem in the Time of Jesus.* Translated by F. H. and C. H. Cave. London: SCM Press, 1985.

Jewish Encyclopedia. Isidore Singer. New York: Funk and Wagnalls, 1905.

Josephus, Flavius. *The Complete Works of Flavius Josephus.* Translated by William Whiston, Grand Rapids: Kregel Publications, 1960.

Keil, Frederic, and Franz Delitzsch. *Old Testament Commentaries.* Reprint. Grand Rapids: Associated Publishers and Authors, n.d.

Lange, John Peter. "Genesis." In *Lange's Commentary on the Holy Scriptures: Critical, Doctrinal and Homiletical.* Translated and edited by Phillip Schaff. Reprint. Grand Rapids: Zondervan, 1864.

————. "The Gospel According to John." In *Lange's Commentary on the Holy Scriptures: Critical, Doctrinal and Homiletical.* Translated and edited by Phillip Schaff. Reprint. Grand Rapids: Zondervan, 1871.

Lenski, R. C. H. *The Interpretation of St. John's Gospel.* 1943. Reprint. Minneapolis: Augsburg, 1961.

Levey, Samson. *The Messiah: An Aramaic Interpretation, The Messianic Exegesis of the Tarqum.* Cincinnati: Hebrew Union College-Jewish Institute of Religion, 1974.

Levy, Shoni, and Sylvia Kaplan. *Guide for the Jewish Homemaker.* New York: Schocken Books, 1964.

Martin, Bernard, *Prayer in Judaism*. New York: Basic Books, 1968.

Montefiore, C. G., and H. Loewe, *Rabbinic Anthology*. New York: Schocken Books, 1974.

Neusner, Jacob. "Judaism in a Time of Crisis." *Judaism*. 21 (Summer 1972).

Patai, Raphael. *The Messiah Texts*. New York: Avon Books, 1979.

Plaut, W. Gunther. *The Growth of Reform Judaism*. Cincinnati: World Union for Progressive Judaism, 1965.

Pool, David de Sola, ed. and trans. *The Traditional Prayer Book for Sabbath and Festivals*. New York: Behrman House, 1960.

Riemer, Jack. "Jewish Reflections on Death." *Illif Review*, 38.

Robertson, A. T. *A Harmony of the Gospels*. New York: Harper and Row, 1950, 1922.

Rosen, Moishe. "Blood Sacrifice." *Jews for Jesus Newsletter*, 11:5746 (1986).

Rosenberg, Roy. "Jesus, Isaac, 'Suffering Servant.' " *Journal of Biblical Literature* 84 (December 1965).

Safrai, S. and M. Stern., eds. *The Jewish People in the First Century*. Vol. 2. Philadelphia: Fortress Press, 1984.

Schuass, Hayyim. *The Jewish Festivals: History and Observance*. Translated by Samuel Jaffe. New York: Schocken Books, 1975.

Schurer, Emil. *The History of the Jewish People in the Age of Jesus Christ*. Edinburgh: T. and T. Clark, 1973.

Siegel, Richard, Sharon Strassfeld, and Michael Strassfeld. *The Jewish Catalog*. Philadelphia: Jewish Publication Society of America, 1973.

Silverman, Morris, ed. *High Holiday Prayer Book*. Hartford: Prayer Book Press, 1951.

Snaith, N. H. *Leviticus and Numbers*. Camden, New Jersey: Thomas Nelson, 1967.

Tenney, Merrill. *The Gospel of John. Expositor's Bible Commentary*. Vol. 9. Grand Rapids: Zondervan, 1981.

Theological Wordbook of the Old Testament. Vol. 1. Edited by R. Laird Harris, Gleason L. Archer, and Bruce K. Waltke. Chicago: Moody, 1980.

The Union Prayer Book for Jewish Worship, rev. ed. Part 2. New York: Central Conference of American Rabbis, 1962.

Urbach, Ephraim E. *The Sages—Their Concepts and Beliefs*. Vols. 1 and 2. Jerusalem: Magnes Press, 1975.

Yoma. Hebrew-English Edition of the Babylonian Talmud. Translated by Leo Jung. London: Soncino Press, 1974.

Zimmerman, Martha. *Celebrate the Feasts*. Minneapolis: Bethany House, 1981.

General Index

Index of Rabbinic References

Index of Apocryphal References

Index of Hebrew Terms

Index of Scripture

1 John		Revelation	
1:7	81	1:13-15	85
1:9	81, 216	11:15	41
2:2	149	11:15-18	41
3:11	149	12:11	81
		21:3-4	212-13

Moody Press, a ministry of the Moody Bible Institute, is designed for education, evangelization, and edification. If we may assist you in knowing more about Christ and the Christian life, please write us without obligation: Moody Press, c/o MLM, Chicago, Illinois 60610.